GUITAR GREATS

GREATS

— OF —

JACKSONVILLE

GUITAR GREATS
— OF —
JACKSONVILLE

MICHAEL RAY FITZGERALD

THE
History
PRESS

Published by The History Press
Charleston, SC
www.historypress.com

First published 2023

Manufactured in the United States

ISBN 9781467153416

Library of Congress Control Number: 2022947994

CONTENTS

MY INITIATION INTO THE CULT

I spent my formative years on a naval air base outside Lemoore, California, about one hundred miles from the Pacific. I discovered a nearby radio station, KLAN-AM, that played every kind of music, from Bobby Bare to James Brown. I loved it all.

My friends and I would go to the on-base cinema for Saturday matinees and then cut over to the enlisted men's cafeteria to drink cherry Cokes and listen to music the "swabbies" selected on the jukebox. Lonnie Mack's "Memphis," a 1963 guitar-driven instrumental version of a Chuck Berry oldie, was a solid favorite.

Gears shifted later that year when I heard "Surfin' USA" by the Beach Boys. That song practically leaped out of the radio's speaker. The Beach Boys combined their love of cars with their music, as they had done with surfing; in fact, the flip side of their first single, "Surfin'," was a car song, "409," a paean to the Chevrolet engine in the 1961 Impala, one of the early muscle cars.

My friend Mike Churchill's mom bought him his first album, the Beach Boys' *Little Deuce Coupe*. We wore that thing out. Churchill and I would grab a floor lamp from his parents' living room, drag it into his bedroom and remove the shade, where it would serve as our imaginary mic stand. Then we would grab tennis rackets for guitars and strum them as we sang along with "Ballad of Ol' Betsy."

Returning home from a Pacific cruise in 1965, my sailor father surprised me with an electric guitar, a cheapo he'd picked up in Japan. "Made in Japan" was not widely considered a mark of quality in those days. The guitar was terrible, its flat-wound strings a quarter inch off the fretboard, much too taut for my twelve-year-old fingers. I didn't even know how to tune it, so I created my own tuning. Befuddled, I started asking my friends who also had electric guitars—I had never even laid eyes on an acoustic guitar—for advice. To my surprise, there were three or four players within a half-mile radius of my house. There was a kid who was a year or two older, Rick Malchow, who was the most advanced. We would gather around, and he would graciously show us beginners how to pick out certain songs.

I discovered that there was a canon of sorts—a set of prerequisites—that beginning players had to master and a recommended order in which to learn them. The following is a partial list:

1. "Little Black Egg" by the Nightcrawlers, a teen group from Daytona Beach, Florida (ninety miles south of Jacksonville).
2. "Gloria" by Them, a white R&B group from Northern Ireland (featuring singer Van Morrison).
3. "Wipeout" by the Surfaris, a surfin' group from Southern California.
4. "Pipeline" by the Chantays, another surfin' group from Southern California.
5. "Hey Joe" by the Leaves, a folk rock group from Los Angeles (based on a version by the Byrds).
6. "House of the Rising Sun" by the Animals, a white R&B group from the north of England.
7. "Walk, Don't Run" by the Ventures from Tacoma, Washington (I had not heard of them at this point but was introduced to their music by another guitar enthusiast).

Many years later, I would find out that young guitarists, roughly my age, from all over the country—even thousands of miles away on the opposite coast—were learning the same tunes.

Even though the Beatles were huge in 1965, one didn't start off with their songs. I suppose we were expected to get the basics down before tackling the heady stuff.

It never occurred to us to form groups, although there was one band at my local junior high school. I suppose we felt we weren't ready. Plus, we didn't even know any drummers or bass players—everyone wanted to play guitar.

There were a couple of teen bands in nearby Lemoore and a couple in neighboring Fresno.

The NightCrawlers, Ltd.

ROBERT KELLY   253-4946
MANAGEMENT   DAYTONA BEACH, FLA

Left: The Nightcrawlers, circa 1965. *Publicity photograph.*

Below: The Daybreakers, Orange Park's premier teen group, 1967. Page Matherson is the second from the left in the back. *Courtesy of Page Matherson.*

Two years later, my dad was transferred to the other side of the continent: Naval Air Station Jacksonville in northeast Florida. I had already heard from a friend who had lived there that the music scene was "happening"—and indeed it was. Compared to California's Central Valley—with the likely exception of Bakersfield, home of the country "honky-tonk" sound—this was the big leagues.

When I got to town in April 1968, there were dozens of working local bands and probably hundreds of guitar players. This was a revelation. In Orange Park—a small, sleepy suburb in nearby Clay County—alone, there were several bands, the most prominent of which was the Daybreakers. That group had a local hit on WAPE-AM, a 50,000-watt "blowtorch" that covered the region from Daytona Beach to the coastal areas of the Carolinas. Thanks to massive airplay, the Daybreakers were booked in and around a 150-mile radius and making boodles.

It just so happened that the group's lead guitarist, Page Matherson, sat in the aisle next to mine in homeroom at Orange Park High. This was inspiring to say the least. Suddenly, it seemed the fantasy could be realized.

Matherson, a navy brat as well, had moved to Orange Park when his father was transferred to NAS Jacksonville when he was ten. He started playing a cheap Japanese electric guitar a year later. Naturally, he began with the basics, such as the Ventures' "Walk, Don't Run" and the Chantays' "Pipeline"—and let's not forget "Little Black Egg." "That was first song the Daybreakers learned," he said.[1]

There were other active groups, such as the Nu-Sounds, the Six Teens and the Sound Vibrations—and that was just in Orange Park. Jacksonville proper had a good dozen or more bands. On any given weekend, my friends and I could cruise a plethora of teen clubs and see live bands everywhere we went. On our side of town, there were the Orange Park Lion's Club, the Sugar Bowl (Twin Hills Civic Association), Woodstock Youth Center and the auditorium at Riverside's Church of the Good Shepherd. It was a teenage music lover's heaven.

The guitar scene in Jacksonville, on the other hand, was not as collegial as the scene in Lemoore. In fact, it was fiercely competitive. Even worse, it was status-conscious; you could not be taken seriously by "real" musicians unless you had a good-quality instrument, and such guys were not generally inclined to give free pointers to beginners.

The underlying metaphysical principle was this: you could not become initiated into the cult without offering a sacrifice of hundreds of dollars to prove your undying commitment. And if you really wanted to demonstrate your eternal vow, you would quit school, burning all your bridges to other career options.

I had to get a good guitar. I harangued my parents until my father finally took me downtown to Paulus Music, which had the local Gibson franchise. I had my heart set on a black Les Paul Custom, like the one Matherson played, but it cost more than $600, which was a fortune in 1969. Fred Paulus, the store owner's son, brought out a 1969 Gibson SG Standard—also designed by Les Paul—which was much lighter and more reasonably priced at $348.40, sales tax included. This was the equivalent of $2,669 in 2022 (the Les Paul Custom I wanted would have been nearly $4,800).[2]

If the SG was good enough for Eric Clapton—Gary Rossington had also purchased one from Fred—it was surely good enough for me. I got a part-time job on base as a busboy and made the twenty-dollar-per-month payments for the guitar. (I quickly learned how to use a mop.) That arrangement didn't last long, however, because the jarheads kept hassling me about my hair, which was maybe an inch over my ears and collar.

I was fascinated with Clapton's work—most of us were—but I could not get the hang of it. I needed help. It never occurred to me to pay for lessons, and I doubt there were any guitar teachers who understood the blues or rock anyway—most teachers were jazzbos. Besides, I couldn't afford lessons, and my parents certainly weren't about to lay out the bucks.

Someone in the trailer park where I lived with my grandmother told me about a guy down the lane who played guitar and was really good. His name was Paul Glass. I took it upon myself to drop in on him. He was maybe a year older than I was and had dropped out of school—thereby burning his career bridges. He was already a part-time professional musician, playing on weekends with Cedar Hills guitarist Jeff Carlisi in a group called Doomsday Refreshment Committee. Both of Paul's parents were at work when I stopped by. He hung out in the trailer all day with the shades drawn, practicing guitar, waiting for his weekend gigs.

I knocked on the door of the trailer. Paul stuck his head out with his long, stringy hair and said brusquely, "What?" I said, "I heard you play guitar." He replied, "Yeah." I raised up the black guitar case I was carrying and said, "Look what I got." He said, "Let me see it." He opened the door, and I followed him inside. It was dark. I pulled the guitar out of its case. As he sat on the couch and played my SG masterfully; he stopped and sneered, "You don't deserve this guitar." I was taken aback at his asperity, but my feelings weren't hurt, because I reckoned this meant I had made a good choice.

Paul Glass (*left*) with Jeff Carlisi in Doomsday Refreshment Committee, 1968. *Courtesy of Jeff Carlisi.*

Glass taught me the secret of playing the blues and rock: super-light-gauge strings, specifically Ernie Ball Extra Extra-Slinkies. Someone with small hands like mine simply could not pull strings the way Clapton did without using super-light strings.[3] This unlocked the door for me, and I spent nearly every night practicing until the wee hours of the morning. I would go back to Glass's trailer many more times with the SG in tow.

Glass, who owned a blond Epiphone Casino (like John Lennon's), wanted to borrow my SG for his gigs. Of course, there was no way I was letting it out of my sight. So, he came up with a plan: I could come along and keep an eye on it. I got to meet and hang out with Carlisi and other musicians from Jacksonville's Westside to see how all this was done. Still, I was not really good enough to play in a band and remained inhibited. Even more daunting, I had no amplifier to speak of—only a tiny, battery-powered practice amp.

I put together a group with some rank beginners like myself, just two guitars and a drummer—no bass player. Without a bassist, you weren't considered a band. We strictly played originals, which was the kiss of death. You could not get gigs without playing certain crowd-pleasers, such as "Mustang Sally." It's funny how that hasn't changed. We wanted to get Glass in the group, but he was out of our league. He came by to jam with us once but never returned.

Even though he wouldn't join our group, I still hung around with Glass, since he lived only a few doors away from me. He taught me about the local guitar culture and its deities. He talked about a group from Daytona called the Allman Joys, which featured Duane Allman, who was considered one of the top players in Florida. Glass insisted, however, that the main man was Dickey Betts, who happened to live in Jacksonville and played around often.

Betts was from Bradenton, south of Tampa. His group, the Blues Messengers, had come to Jacksonville the previous year to work as the house band at a nightclub called the Scene. The club's owner asked the group to change its name to the Second Coming, as bassist Berry Oakley looked like Jesus with his long hair and beard.[4]

Glass and I journeyed all over the area to see Betts at every opportunity. One night we hitchhiked to a Westside district called Paxon to see the Second Coming at the Woodstock Youth Center on Beaver Street. This was a rather rough, working-class area, and with our long hair—Glass's hair was nearly

Dickey Betts with the Second Coming, 1968. *Photograph by Allen Facemire; used with permission.*

down to his shoulders—we had to avoid the local rednecks, which is pretty difficult since we stood out on the street with our thumbs sticking out. When we saw a muscle car coming, we would duck back onto the sidewalk and look the other way.

Admission was a bit steep—two dollars.[5] We couldn't wait to hear Betts play "Crossroads." Betts could have given Clapton a run for his money. But to our dismay, Betts didn't play many solos that night. A diffident young man with stringy, blondish hair was "sitting in" on guitar and hogging the solos.

We were irate. "Let Dickey play!" we shouted. "We came to hear Dickey!"

We were heckling Duane Allman. Even though Glass had mentioned Allman to me, he didn't recognize the guitarist staring down at his guitar with his hair in his face.

Another local legend was Larry Reinhardt, who, like Betts, came from the Tampa Bay region. In fact, Reinhardt had himself been a member of the Blues Messengers (the Second Coming's earlier name) but had split off to form his own group, a power trio called the Load, which included Richard Price on bass.[6] While Betts did his best Clapton imitations, Reinhardt specialized in Hendrix's style. Both groups would often appear on the same shows, since they shared a manager, Allen Facemire. Facemire had his own Sunday night program on the Big Ape called *The Underground Circus*, on which he would play the latest psychedelic sounds.

Sweet Rooster, 1970. *Left to right*: Ken Lyons, Bill Pelkey, Donnie Van Zant, Jeff Carlisi and Kevin Elson. *Courtesy of Jeff Carlisi.*

A year or so after meeting Jeff Carlisi and going to gigs with him and Glass, I got a call from him inviting me to come over to audition for a new group he was forming with Donnie Van Zant, Ronnie's younger brother (Lynyrd Skynyrd was not yet signed to a major label). Their group was called Sweet Rooster. They had a keyboardist, Kevin Elson on Hammond organ, and were doing two or three Allman Brothers Band numbers, along with some songs by an obscure group called Illinois Speed Press.

Knowing the prestige value of having good equipment—sometimes you could get a gig by simply having the right gear—I borrowed a Marshall half stack from my friend Caleb Massee and headed over to Cedar Hills to Elson's parents' garage. I didn't get the gig, but that was okay by me; I didn't much care for the material and could not seem to rise to the task. I was into Sly Stone and Ray Charles and wanted to play more R&B.

Three of the members of Sweet Rooster, Carlisi, Van Zant and bassist Ken Lyons, would go on to form 38 Special, a guitar-driven group that would score no less than fifteen top-forty hits in the coming decades. Carlisi's solo on 38 Special's "Hold on Loosely" would cement his status as a guitar god. There was also a point when he may have been considered as a replacement for Ed King in Lynyrd Skynyrd.[7]

CULT OF THE KITHARA

J immy Page, Jeff Beck, Eric Clapton, Jimi Hendrix, Eddie Van Halen—there's a reason these great players are often referred to as "guitar gods." The guitar has always been imbued with a sacred aura, and these men—for some perhaps unknown reason, there are few women players of note—know how to wield it with maximum effect.

The electric guitar, wrote Thomas Dunne, "became an icon of American culture, as it transcended its original purpose of merely producing musical sound."[8]

> *The refinement and improvements in amplification in the 1960s allowed guitarists to play at tremendous volume. Those who could harness that volume and create amazing sounds while demonstrating remarkable skill as lead guitarists came to be venerated, even worshipped.*[9]

The guitar was mystical from its beginnings: the kithara (an ancestor of the guitar), the lyre and other stringed instruments that the ancient Greeks and Romans said were used—if not created—by the sun god Apollo, who was also the god of poetry. Historian Mark Cartwright wrote, "Playing the kithara was an important part of any young Greek male's education."[10]

During the European Middle Ages, the guitar accompanied traveling troubadours, who sang of current events, as well as themes of chivalry and courtly love.

A statue of Apollo playing a kithara. Hall of Muses, Museo Pio-Clementino, Vatican City. *From Wikipedia.*

> *They were responsible for entertaining the nobility of the region and traveled from city to city performing various songs and epic poetry for all classes of audiences. Troubadours were the primary source of secular music for audiences during the medieval period....Far removed from the influence of the Catholic Church, troubadours were able to create material and disseminate information without moral constraints and expectations.*[11]

The troubadour tradition eventually found its way to the American South and was embodied in folk singers like Woody Guthrie from Oklahoma and in blues singers like Charlie Patton and Robert Johnson, both from Mississippi. Further demonstrating the guitar's supernatural mystique, Johnson's guitar wizardry was rumored to have been gained by making a midnight deal with the devil.[12]

Despite the devil's contribution, playing the guitar has long been seen as a gentlemanly pastime—even as a respectable profession—in the South. During the region's hot summers, men and women—mostly men—would gather on their porches and play guitars, banjoes and fiddles, sometimes passing a jug for inspiration. Some even managed to make a living at it.

Why does the guitar itself seem gendered—a male thing? There is "some kind of male virility attached to the guitar," guitarist Diane Ponzio told a *Washington Post* reporter. "We're supposed to hang languorously over our boyfriends as they play those power chords."[13]

In her autobiography—referring to her teenage years in the late 1960s and early 1970s, when such idolatry was cresting—singer-guitarist Chrissy Hynde of the Pretenders wrote:

> *We were the new generation of guitar worshippers. We were taking up philosophies from what we could interpret of the musings of twenty-three-year-old guitar players. Electric guitar was the Holy Grail, the pinnacle of our culture; we thought anyone who could play like Rick Derringer or Johnny Winter was touched by divinity.*[14]

No one made the electric guitar seem so utterly phallic as Jimi Hendrix in the late 1960s—except perhaps David Bowie, who, in the early 1970s, would simulate fellatio on guitarist Mick Ronson onstage during a particularly incendiary solo.

Perhaps the absurdity of such gendered images contributed to a decline of the electric guitar in pop music. "While sexism is impossible to measure, it reaches beyond media, advertising and products and pervades guitar culture itself."[15] From 2008 to 2018, sales of electric guitars dropped from 1.5 million per year to slightly more than 1 million per year, a decline of more than 30 percent. Especially with the advent of hip-hop, "guitar-driven music isn't nearly as relevant as it used to be."[16] In 2017, the *Washington Post* declared the "slow, secret death of the six-string electric." YouTuber Rick Beato said, "There hasn't been a rock guitar hero since Synyster Gates in Avenged Sevenfold."[17] Also in 2017, guitar god Eric Clapton lamented, "Maybe the guitar is over." Yet, by 2020, guitar sales were climbing again, nearly half of these sales coming from women.[18]

Unfortunately, it's obvious that Jacksonville's electric guitar scene was—and still is—not only a boys' club but also a white boys' club. It was next to impossible to find any famous Black players—or even more than a handful of Black guitarists at all—while researching this book. There were many great Black guitarists in cities such as Chicago, Detroit, Memphis and Philadelphia, but in Jacksonville, they are extremely rare for whatever reasons. Jacksonville's Blind Blake (Arthur Phelps) went on to national success in the 1920s, signing with Chicago-based Paramount Records, but the electric guitar would not be invented until a decade later. The only prominent Black electric guitarist I could find was Guitar Redd (Herman Gissendanner), who started off as a backing musician for the Atlanta-based R&B group the Tams and went on to work with a band who backed the Shirelles, along with Dorothy Moore and other singers.

Once a staple of R&B, soul and funk, the electric guitar is essentially invisible in hip-hop. And it's hard to even find one in pop music these days. It seems the only genres in which the electric guitar survives are country and heavy metal.

Is there a future for the electric guitar? Will it make a comeback? We must leave such questions up in the air for now. So let us take a trip back to 1960, when the electric guitar came to Jacksonville, Florida, and ate the brains of its youth—well, the boys' brains anyway.

1

IT CAME FROM CALIFORNIA

*I*n 1960, the pop charts were clogged with saccharine pretty-boys like Neil Sedaka, Bobby Vee, Frankie Avalon and—let's not forget—Jacksonville's own Johnny Tillotson.

Out of nowhere, the Ventures hit like a tsunami.

The electric guitar began replacing toy machine guns as the hottest new fad item for boys, just as the Barbie doll did for girls. The electric guitar—as an icon of western culture—might have even been one of the U.S. state department's secret weapons in beating back communism.[19]

The electric guitar epidemic had actually been gathering for decades, pioneered by jazz greats Charlie Christian, Les Paul, Barney Kessel and others. The instrument also became an integral component of country music among major players like Nashville's Chet Atkins and Hank Garland, along with Bakersfield's Buck Owens and Don Rich. Black guitarists, such as Chuck Berry, Bo Diddley and Freddie King, embraced the electric guitar; it was de rigeur in Chicago-style (electrified) blues bands.

The electric guitar played a big part in rockabilly, a hybrid of country and upbeat blues. Elvis Presley's guitarist Scotty Moore was an early rockabilly idol in 1954, and his psychobilly solo on "Too Much" (1956) would become a touchstone. Bill Haley's Comets featured an impressive solo by Danny Cedrone on their 1955 hit "Rock around the Clock," which was more or less a remake of Hank Williams's 1947 hit "Move It on Over," which also featured a jazzy electric solo by Zeke Turner.

In 1958, it became apparent that the electric guitar was a powerful entity that could be used for good or evil. In Fredericksburg, Virginia, Link Wray literally drove teens crazy with a controversial instrumental titled "Rumble," which alarmed civic leaders and radio programmers, who assumed the song may have been an incitement to riot or at least a contributing factor in "juvenile delinquency" (the term *rumble* was gang slang for a street fight).[20] That same year, Duane Eddy took the fetishization of the electric guitar even further with "Rebel Rouser." He also had a hit the following year with "Peter Gunn," a guitar-drenched rendition of Henry Mancini's theme from the popular TV series.

England and Europe jumped on the electric guitar bandwagon. In early 1960, British guitarist Bert Weedon recorded "Apache," which was soon covered by the Shadows, featuring Hank Marvin, who would go on to become a UK legend. However, the most successful version of the tune was recorded later that year by Danish jazz guitarist Jørgen Ingmann and released a year later in the United States by Atlantic Records. While Weedon's original version of "Apache" sounded like something from a spaghetti western, Ingmann's version evinced a faux flamenco rhythm guitar behind two electric guitars—one low, another high—in a sort of call and response. It was a guitar smorgasbord, and it shot to number two in *Billboard*'s pop chart.

Also in 1960, a quartet from Tacoma, Washington, remade a 1954 tune by jazz guitarist Johnny Smith called "Walk, Don't Run." The song had also been recorded in 1957 by Chet Atkins. The Ventures' rock 'n' roll adaptation would become a classic, as well as a staple in every young guitarist's repertoire.

The Ventures, formed in 1958, started out as a guitar duo called the Versatones, comprising Don Wilson on rhythm guitar and Bob Bogle on lead. Both started out on ten-dollar pawnshop guitars.[21]

Nokie Edwards had played guitar with Buck Owens but was performing on bass when the duo first heard him. He was recruited as a bass player, but after hearing him on guitar, Bogle decided that they should switch instruments.[22] Two years later, the Ventures' version of "Walk, Don't Run" would rocket to number two on *Billboard*'s Hot 100, but the band's importance cannot be assayed by its chart position alone. The Ventures were indubitably "the band that launched a thousand bands."[23]

The Ventures certainly lit a fire under many aspiring young guitarists all over the world, not least among them Jacksonville's Walter Eaton. At one point, Eaton said he and his group "learned every song the Ventures ever recorded."[24]

Early on, by his own admission, Eaton had little talent on the instrument. He felt his only option—since no local band would have him—was to form his own group, which he dubbed Leroy and the Monarchs (Leroy being Eaton's middle name). Eaton was savvy enough to work with a slightly more talented guitarist: his thirteen-year-old neighbor Jimmy Amerson.[25] "When Jimmy and I started out, we couldn't play anything," Eaton said. "But he learned faster than I did."[26]

Back in Los Angeles, Dick Dale, a son of Middle Eastern immigrants who had moved from Massachusetts to Southern California, had taken Duane Eddy's guitar mystique a step or two further; he turned the electric guitar into a sort of voodoo talisman. An avid surfer, Dale combined his love for the sport with his love for the electric guitar, reinventing it as a symbol of beach culture while styling himself "king of the surf guitar."

Dale's first single, released on his own Del-Tone label in 1961, was "Let's Go Trippin'," widely considered the first "surf-rock" hit. "Let's Go Trippin'" was a simple, three-chord rock 'n' roll number that peaked at number sixty in early 1962. Its significance, however, cannot be gauged by its chart position. The surfin' sound had taken the electric guitar to exciting new vistas and inspired dozens of young bands. For one example, a section of "Let's Go Trippin'" became the foundation for the 1963 instrumental hit "Wipe Out" by the Surfaris, which, in turn, became a standard item in any budding guitarist's repertoire and a staple of garage bands nationwide.

Dale, a lefty who played a Fender Stratocaster—made in Southern California—might have gotten the idea to do something similar to "Apache" when he recorded "Misirlou," a ubiquitous Middle Eastern folk melody that had been done as a pop record in 1946 by pianist Jan August. Dale's 1962 version was heavy on sixteenth-note tremolo runs and got him a good deal of attention as a guitar wizard—the Eddie Van Halen of his era.

Dale inspired countless guitarists, including Carl Wilson, whose group, the Beach Boys, would figure out how to combine Dale's surfin' sound—which was entirely instrumental and guitar-based—with pop songcraft. The Beach Boys did remakes of both "Let's Go Trippin'" and "Misirlou."

Surfing became—and still is—a popular sport in Florida, even though the waves there are not half as big as those on the West Coast. The surfin' sound became the soundtrack of the "salt life." It also became an inspiration for hundreds of Florida guitarists who busied themselves learning "Walk, Don't Run," "Wipe Out" and "Pipeline," a 1962 hit from the California group the Chantays.[27] These tunes became not only standards in the surf-music canon but also mandatory items for any students of the electric guitar.

One such guitarist, Charles "Tiny" Tackle, from Jacksonville's Northside (not far from Eaton's neighborhood), would get so good at replicating Dick Dale's sound and style that he formed his own group called, appropriately, Tiny and the Surfers. This was not an exclusively instrumental group, however, as Tackle also provided vocals. The Surfers included Gary Hadden (Tackle's half brother) on rhythm guitar, Norman Ford on bass, John Roberts on drums and Donn Finney on saxophone, an instrument not generally associated with the surfin' sound (but it had been featured in Duane Eddy's music). This group would, in turn, inspire many other groups.

There was a country picker on the *Jimmy Strickland Show* on WJXT-TV named Wendell Griffin who was a local favorite. However, it appears that in the early 1960s, Jacksonville had no Big Kahuna on electric guitar—no Dick Dale–style figurehead leaving imitators in his wake. Tiny Tackle may have been the closest thing, but he himself was a Dale acolyte. It appears that most local guitarists were inspired by out-of-towners.[28] Jimmy Amerson was inspired by a Bradenton guitarist named Jimmy Paramore, who came to Jacksonville to perform at Westside's Forrest Inn (only blocks away from where Lynyrd Skynyrd would be formed a few years later).[29] Dickey Betts, also from Bradenton, had been inspired by Paramore.[30] Betts himself would become the reigning "guitar god" of Jacksonville when his group the Second Coming moved to town in 1968.

Jacksonville's Northside was a hot spot for young musicians. There were several young groups in the area, notably the Redcoats, the Echoes, the Vikings (who, at one point, included future Allman Brothers Band drummer Claude "Butch" Trucks), Tiny and the Surfers and Leroy the Monarchs.

The Monarchs, led by guitarist Walter Eaton, evolved into the Classics with the addition of singing drummer Dennis Yost, who came from the Echoes. Abandoning the guitar fad and turning to a more easy-listening style, the Classics would later strike pay dirt with "Spooky," which went to number two on *Billboard's* Hot 100 in early 1968, proving that a combination of talent, hard work and dedication could lead to fame and fortune—an escape from workaday drudgery—even in a predominantly blue-collar city like Jacksonville, where such fantasies were generally discouraged.

Guitar fever would take hold of the region. Jacksonville would eventually assume its place alongside Los Angeles, London, Detroit, Chicago, Nashville, Memphis and Muscle Shoals as one of the great guitar towns. The list of famous guitarists who lived and worked in Jacksonville would grow to include:

- J.R. Cobb (Classics IV, Atlanta Rhythm Section and the Highwaymen).
- Jimmy Amerson (Mike Pinera and Freddy Fender).
- Jimmy Pitman (Nightcrawlers, Strawberry Alarm Clock and Jumbo).
- Auburn Burrell (session player in Atlanta and Los Angeles).
- Robert Conti (notable jazz player in Los Angeles).
- Gary Starling (Doug Carn Trio).
- Dickey Betts (Allman Brothers Band and Great Southern).
- Duane Allman (cofounder and leader of the Allman Brothers Band and also a notable session player in Muscle Shoals and New York).
- Dru Lombar (Grinderswitch).
- Scott Boyer (Cowboy).
- Tommy Talton (Cowboy).
- Allen Collins (Lynyrd Skynyrd and Rossington Collins Band).
- Ed King (Lynyrd Skynyrd and Strawberry Alarm Clock).
- Steve Gaines (Lynyrd Skynyrd).
- Jeff Carlisi (38 Special).
- Dave Hlubek (Molly Hatchet).
- Duane Roland (Molly Hatchet).
- Bobby Ingram (Molly Hatchet).
- Mike Owings (Allen Collins Band, Molly Hatchet and David Allan Coe).
- Ron Perry (China Sky).
- Page Matherson (the Daybreakers and Richfield).
- Jim Harrison (Richfield).
- Erik Lundgren (Johnny Van Zant Band and Molly Hatchet).
- Mike Campbell (Mudcrutch, Tom Petty and the Heartbreakers, Fleetwood Mac and Dirty Knobs).
- Danny Roberts (Mudcrutch and Derek Trucks Band).
- John Philip Kurzweg (Atlantic recording artist).
- Ace Moreland (blues singer and guitarist with King Snake Records).
- Greg Baril (Greg Baril Band, Derek Trucks Band and Artimus Pyle Band).
- Randall Hall (Lynyrd Skynyrd reunion and Allen Collins Band).
- Derek Trucks (Allman Brothers Band, Derek Trucks Band and Tedeschi Trucks Band).

- Susan Tedeschi (Susan Tedeschi Band and Tedeschi Trucks Band).
- Wes Borland (Limp Bizkit and Big Dumb Face).
- Brian Liesegang (Filter and Nine Inch Nails).
- Jasin Todd (Shinedown, Fuel, Maylene and the Sons of Disaster).
- Kenny and Denny Scott (Swirl 360).
- Damien Starkey (Burn Season and Puddle of Mudd).
- Ben Harper (Yellowcard).
- Paul Phillips (Puddle of Mudd).
- Josh Burke (Red Jumpsuit Apparatus).

2

CLASSICS FOUR AND MORE

Walter Eaton was a fifteen-year-old Jackson High School student when he got bit by the guitar bug. It happened when he heard the Ventures' 1960 hit "Walk, Don't Run" on the radio. He already had a box guitar but desperately wanted an electric. He begged his mother to buy him a Sears Silvertone. She did.

Eaton's first attempt to become a professional musician came when he hounded a Northside group called the Echoes, which included guitarist Jimmy Sigg, into giving him an audition. But he just wasn't good enough, he said.[31] The Echoes included another Jackson High student, drummer Dennis Yost, who would later play a big part in Eaton's career.

Jacksonville's Northside was the hot spot for modern music in those days, according to Eaton. He said, "The first bands of any consequence in town were the Redcoats and the Echoes."

Eaton worked after school at a local drugstore named Brentwood Sundries, which most everyone usually referred to as "Miz Lowe's." The drugstore, like many of its day, contained a soda shop that welcomed local kids, who would sit at the counter and slurp ice cream sodas and socialize. Eaton was the soda jerk. He sometimes brought his acoustic guitar to work with him so he could practice during his breaks.

Jimmy Amerson and Ty Branch, both budding guitarists who lived in the nearby Brentwood projects, were all of thirteen when they walked over to Miz Lowe's after school. Eaton was out front picking when the two sauntered over and struck up a conversation with him about guitars. The

Leroy and the Monarchs, 1961. *Left to right*: Burt Norton, Walter Eaton, Bobby Bowen, Glen Futch and Greg Carol. *Courtesy of Walter Eaton.*

three decided to get together at Eaton's house to practice and teach each other. "We initiated a running contest to see who could play the most songs," Eaton said. "Jimmy was learning faster than I was."[32]

Amerson picked up a Supro electric soon after and carried it and a tiny amp on foot to Eaton's house on a regular basis.[33] They practiced together in Eaton's family's backyard. Sometimes, they would go to a nearby coin laundromat and unplug one of the washers to get electricity.[34]

Eaton decided it would be a cool thing to form a group. Eaton christened the group Leroy and the Monarchs—Leroy was Eaton's middle name. He thought it sounded slightly snazzier than Walter and the Monarchs.[35] Amerson didn't think much of the name. He told Eaton the group needed a better name, "something classic."[36]

By 1961, Amerson was gone. His parents had moved to the Paxon District in the city's Westside, where he attended Paxon Junior High. There, he met guitarist James "J.R." Cobb, as well as drummer Robert Nix, both of whom graduated from Paxon High in 1962. Amerson wanted to get into a group. He approached Cobb, who was working at a Pantry Pride store. When Classics members Glen Futch (bass) and Bobby Bowen (drums) heard about the new group, the Emeralds, being formed, they called Amerson, telling him they wanted in. "I basically stole them from Walter's group," Amerson quipped.[37] The Emeralds soon started getting some paying gigs in teen clubs.

Another Paxon student, guitarist-singer Jimmy Pitman, started showing up at the Emeralds' gigs and sitting in with the group. The other members liked his playing, plus he sang a lot, so he was invited to perform whenever he was available.[38] Pitman and Amerson spent hours together learning Freddie King's 1961 R&B hit "Hideaway." Amerson said, "We put every dime we had in that jukebox so we could learn that song."[39] Pitman would also sit in at gigs with the Classics. A couple years later, he

Left: The Emeralds at Woodstock Youth Center, circa 1963. *Left to right*: Glen Futch, Bobby Bowen, J.R. Cobb and Jimmy Amerson. *Courtesy of Jimmy Amerson.*

Below: Mike West and the Motions, circa 1965. Mike Pinera (*left*) and Jimmy Amerson (*second from the left*). *Photograph courtesy of Mike Pinera; used with permission.*

turned up in Daytona Beach, where he was recruited as a replacement member of the Nightcrawlers.

Amerson kept the Emeralds going until he filled in one night for a missing lead guitarist in the Tampa group the Motions, led by singer-guitarist Mike Pinera. The Motions were performing at the Comic Book Club, and Pinera hired him on the spot. "Jimmy is a very talented player," Pinera said.[40] Amerson toured with that group until early 1966, when he got drafted and sent to Vietnam. Amerson said it took him a long time to recuperate from the trauma he experienced during the war.[41] He eventually returned to the music scene, making himself known as one of the finest players in town.[42]

Amerson moved to Atlanta in the 1970s; there, he hooked up with Classics comanager Alan Diggs, who was, by this time, running his own agency. Diggs put him on the circuit with a couple of touring rock bands. After a brief return to Jacksonville, he went back to Atlanta to work at a cowboy bar called Country Roads, where he met singer Freddy Fender. He toured with Fender for about eight months until he realized Fender wasn't going to use him on any of his recording sessions.[43] Amerson then took a house gig at a popular Atlanta nightspot called Southern Comfort, where, over the course of sixteen years, he backed Narvel Felts, Ace Cannon, the Coasters and the Drifters, remaining there until he retired in 2014.[44]

The sudden loss of three members of the Classics left Walter Eaton in the lurch. Undeterred, Eaton got to work forming a revamped version of the group featuring himself as lead singer and rhythm guitarist. One secret to his success was his adaptability. He was willing to change musicians, styles— whatever it took.

Bassist Futch was replaced by Amerson's pal Ty Branch. Paxon High graduate Robert Nix replaced Bobby Bowen, who'd gotten drafted, on drums.[45] Nix stayed for about a year before he left to join Susan (Robey) and the Dynamics, a group that included siblings Willie (also known as "Shink") and Charlie Morrison on guitars.[46]

In 1964, Dennis Yost, the drummer for the Echoes, had a falling out with that group, so he came aboard the Classics. Few people knew Yost could sing. Eaton recalled, "One night, while Dennis and I were driving home from a gig, he started singing along with the car radio."[47] Eaton phased himself out as the group's lead singer, handing the vocal reins over to Yost, who remained on drums—standing up—while singing.

The Classics graduated from teen clubs to playing six nights a week in smoky nightclubs. At this point, they abandoned their ambitions as a guitar group and entered their lounge-lizard phase, which would serve them well. They began performing as the house band at the Golden Gate, a favorite hangout for sailors, where they proved to be a big draw. Eaton talked owner Lou Ingle into financing a single, which was recorded that year at Sound Laboratory on nearby Edgewood Avenue and released on, appropriately, Golden Gate Records.[48]

These two songs, "Cry Me a Tear" and "Who's That New Guy," both written by Eaton, were throwbacks to the doo-wop era and a far cry from the guitar instrumentals Leroy and the Monarchs used to perform. Eaton had switched the focus of the group from guitars to vocals, so the members worked hard on their harmonies. There were no guitar solos, but Eaton's rhythm guitar is high in the mix. Yost's lead vocals display little of the polish he would latter attain; it's probably just as well that his voice is buried in the muddy mixes.[49]

Eaton got into a beef with the club's manager and quit the group. He landed a day job working for the city and recommended J.R. Cobb from the Emeralds as his replacement, along with a second guitarist, Joe Wilson, another Jackson High graduate who doubled on keyboards.

Cobb had not been making much money as a musician and had taken a day job as an apprentice welder. "When I told my mother I planned to [become a full-time musician], she said, 'I hope you don't think you can make a living doing that.'" However, after joining the Classics, he began making twice as much playing music as he had been while working at Florida Steel.[50] Cobb and Wilson also landed a three-week stint backing Jacksonville singer Connie Haines in Vegas.[51]

The Classics broke up a few months after Eaton left, but Cobb and Yost went back to Eaton, wanting to put the group together again.[52] Eaton quit his day job, and the Classics were retooled as a four-piece band with Eaton, Cobb, Yost and Wilson. Again, the group found itself with three guitarists, so Eaton switched to bass and Wilson to Farfisa organ.

In early 1965, the Classics were in nearby Daytona Beach, where they served as a backup band and opening act for rockabilly singer Billy "Crash" Craddock at a new club called the Neptune a-Go-Go inside the Daytona Plaza Hotel. The owner liked the band and offered its members a steady gig, which they jumped at. While the group was working in Daytona, a pair of local guitarists, siblings Duane and Gregg Allman—who had their own popular group, the Allman Joys—came over and sat in.

A man walked in who would change their lives forever: a part-time talent agent and manager from the Lowery Organization, Alan Diggs. Diggs, a former New Port Richey police officer, had been comanaging Tommy Roe's backing band, the Roemans (bassist Berry Oakley, later a member of the Second Coming and a founding member of the Allman Brothers Band, would join the Roemans in 1966). He was so impressed by the Classics—who were a very tight, polished act by this point—that he invited them to come to Atlanta to make a record.[53]

The Classics IV were assigned to Lowery writer/producer Joe South, a seasoned session guitarist and songwriter (who played the opening riff on

Aretha Franklin's version of "Chain of Fools" and would have hits of his own). South contributed his song "Pollyanna," which had been recorded in 1965 by Lowery talent Billy Joe Royal and published by Lowery Music.

Historians White and Williams remarked, "It was so imitative of the Four Seasons, it sounded almost like a parody."[54] The B side was "Cry Baby," written by Cobb and also published by Lowery. It, too, was an unabashed Four Seasons knockoff with a jarring, out-of-tune, distorted guitar solo by Cobb. The single stiffed. In addition, they received a cease-and-desist letter from an established doo-wop group in New York named the Classics, so a name change was in order. Lowery himself suggested the Classics IV, there being four members.[55]

Only slightly deterred, the Classics IV went back into Mastersound Studio (of which Lowery was co-owner) and recorded a remake of the Diamonds' 1957 doo-wop hit "Little Darlin'." Once again, they made the song sound like a Four Seasons recording. This, the group's second major-label release, also stiffed. Things weren't looking good.

J.R. Cobb, always looking for ways to expand his horizons, started writing songs with comanager Buddy Buie, who had also been managing the Candymen (Roy Orbison's backing band, for which Cobb's Jacksonville buddy Robert Nix was the drummer). Buie and Cobb took a "lite" jazz tune by saxophonist Mike Sharpe (Shapiro) that had reached the lower rungs of the charts and wrote some lyrics for it. It was, conveniently, owned by Lowery Music. The Classics IV went back into the studio, this time with Buie as producer, and recorded "Spooky." Rebuffed by Capitol Records, Lowery got Los Angeles–based Imperial Records to pick the single up. By February 1968, "Spooky" had risen to the number-three position on *Billboard*'s pop chart.[56]

"Spooky" was a breakthrough for the Classics, and it took the members to the big-time. They toured all over the United States and appeared on important TV shows, like Dick Clark's *American Bandstand*. But it's not enough to reach the top rungs, you've got to find a way to stay there. After releasing two more singles that stiffed, Cobb became convinced that the Classics IV were one-hit wonders and that it was over.[57] He decided he wanted to focus on songwriting and studio work, so he quit the Classics IV. But he continued to cowrite songs for the group.

Between stints on the road, Eaton worked as a recording engineer at Jacksonville's Sound Lab. Dennis Yost did some session work there as well as a drummer and vocalist. He played drums on the Daybreakers' 1967–68 singles that created a regional buzz on WAPE. Eaton was the sound engineer on these recordings and also wrote string arrangements.

Classics IV, 1968. *Left to right*: David Phillips, Walter Eaton, Mack Doss and Dennis Yost. *Publicity photograph; courtesy of Walter Eaton.*

Eaton was in the studio when he heard guitarist Mack Doss, who had recently arrived from Bradenton, playing on a demo session. Doss was good friends with Dickey Betts. The two had even played together in the Thunderbeats, in which Betts subbed for the underage Larry Reinhardt on school nights. Betts, who had been coming to Jacksonville since 1965 to perform—he had once led the house band at the Westside's Normandy Lounge—advised Doss that if he wanted regular work as a musician, he should move to Jacksonville. So he did.

Eaton and Yost assembled a new four-piece lineup with Doss and Doss's friend from Ocala keyboardist David Phillips. This configuration lasted about six months. Imperial Records had released "Stormy"—also sounding remarkably like "Spooky"—which hit *Billboard's* number-five spot. Lightning struck again. However, Doss felt the group was locked into a lounge-like, easy-listening style he didn't care for; he wanted to play psychedelic rock like his friends Betts and Reinhardt.[58] But hey, it was steady work.

Meanwhile, Cobb and Wilson were working with another group in an Atlanta lounge when "Stormy" broke. The Classic IV's managers decided it would be a good idea to put the original group back together, so Eaton had to let Doss and Phillips go. Doss returned to Jacksonville to become a mainstay on the area's music scene for decades.

Yost was put out front so he could move around the stage, and drummer Kim Venable was added to the lineup. The group was then renamed Dennis Yost and the Classics IV.

J.R. Cobb's heart wasn't in it. After a brief period, he quit again and decided to stay in Atlanta, where he and Buie continued writing songs. They soon scored another hit, "Be Young, Be Foolish but Be Happy," with the Tams, another Lowery-affiliated act.

In the coming year, Buie—with backing from Lowery—decided to build his own studio, Studio One, in Doraville and begin assembling a house band that included Cobb and drummer Robert Nix. This band was dubbed the

Atlanta Rhythm Section, which, after bringing in singer Rodney Justo from Tampa, went on to sign with MCA Records and score several hits.

Cobb's final exit from the Classics necessitated yet another replacement. Jacksonville guitarist Auburn Burrell, then only seventeen years old, lived about a mile from Sound Lab Studio and was a first-call session player there.

Burrell was considered among the best players in town by many of his peers.[59] Jimmy Amerson said, "Auburn has always been a prime-time player."[60] Page Matherson of the Daybreakers, who studied with Burrell—Burrell had played on a Daybreakers session at Sound Lab—said Burrell was a prodigy. "He had amazing chops, even then; plus, he had a distinctive style."[61]

Burrell started out on acoustic guitar at the age of eleven but was attracted to the electric when he heard the Ventures and Duane Eddy. His earliest local hero was Paxon resident Jimmy Pitman. "He was a hell of a player and taught me a lot of stuff."

Burrell sometimes sneaked into the Golden Gate Lounge to hear Shink Morrison with Susan and the Dynamics. "[Morrison] was an unbelievable player and a big influence on me." Burrell also followed Tiny Tackle of Tiny and the Surfers, along with Tackle's half brother, Gary Hadden, who played with the Vikings with drummer Butch Trucks. Other players he admired were jazz guitarist Ray Holmes, who worked at Marvin Kay's music store, and jazz player Buddy Pitts (Pitts was a co-owner of Sound Lab Recording Studio and later became secretary-treasurer of Musician's Local 444).[62] Burrell said he was in Marvin Kay's one time when Pitts and Robert Conti, who came to Jacksonville in 1966, were jamming on a thirty-two-bar blues and "blew everyone away." Burrell bought a 1955 Telecaster that had belonged to Conti and began taking lessons from him.[63]

By the age of sixteen, Burrell had hooked up with a prominent Jacksonville group called the Dalton Gang, which was managed by WPDQ jock Dino Summerlin and featured on a 1967 TV show called *Shakin' Up Summer*. The group released a single, a cover of Marvin Gaye's "Stubborn Kind of Fellow," on Summerlin's Kimberly Ann Records. Singer and former session guitarist Joe South came to Jacksonville for a couple of performances and was backed by the Dalton Gang. "He [South] became a huge influence on me," Burrell recalled.[64] The other guitarist in the Daltons was Rick Foxworth, an impressive player in his own right.[65]

Burrell mentioned two Black players, "Five-String Otis" (whose real name he cannot recall) and Neil Seltzer of the R&B group the Lemon Twisters, who played with finger picks. "He was a monster," Burrell said. The Lemon Twisters recorded one single with promoter Tommy Register's R&D label.

The Lemon Twisters, circa 1965. Neil Seltzer is the second from the left on the back row. *R&D Records publicity photograph; courtesy of Tom Register.*

Burrell speculates that there may not have been many Black guitarists who gained much exposure in Jacksonville. The city was segregated in those days; if there were any other great Black players, he said he didn't know of them.[66]

Burrell also listened a lot to J.R. Cobb, whom he thinks is an underrated player: "Most people don't know what a monster he was." In 1968, Eaton asked Burrell to come to Atlanta to replace Cobb in the Classics. Burrell's tenure with the group lasted less than two years. The group toured relentlessly, he said. "We did 265 dates in one twelve-month period."[67] There was some kind of management shake-up, and he and drummer Kim Venable were let go.

Burrell hooked up with Atlanta singer Mylon LeFevre, a Christian rocker whose family owned a recording studio. In 1970, Burrell worked on two of LeFevre's albums, the first of which appeared with Atlantic's Cotillion subsidiary and the second with Columbia. Burrell served as LeFevre's bandleader until LeFevre dissolved his band.

Tired of the road, Burrell decided to stay in Atlanta and concentrate on session work. He worked with the likes of Joe South and Mac Davis (both Lowery clients), among others. In 1972, Ilene Berns, songwriter Bert Berns's widow, decided to relocate her operation from New York to Atlanta. Burrell became a member of Berns's studio band at her Web IV Studio, where he, alongside keyboardist-guitarist Joe Wilson from Jacksonville, worked with Paul Davis, Allen Toussaint, Peabo Bryson, Billy Joe Royal and others.

In the mid-1970s, Burrell, worried that the Atlanta studio scene might be drying up, took the great leap to Los Angeles, where he knew a former Atlanta studio operator who did jingle work. Burrell landed a day job remodeling an old studio that had been purchased by producer Richard Perry. When Perry heard Burrell play, he hired him to work with Leo Sayer.

In Los Angeles, Burrell also worked with Frankie Miller, David Blue, Burton Cummings and others. In 1984, he got a call from Mac Davis and spent six years in his band, appearing on the *Tonight Show* a dozen times.

Expanding his skill set, Burrell started engineering sessions and, in 1992, produced some demos for Los Angeles rock band Rage Against the Machine. Two of the songs he engineered landed on the group's Epic Records debut.[68] Tired of the rat race, Burrell finally gave up on the music business, went back to school and started training horses. He now lives in Colorado and still plays a bit for fun.[69]

J.R. COBB MAY HAVE left the Classics IV in 1968—and again in 1969—but he continued to provide the hits. For Cobb, there was more money in writing songs than playing guitar. The group had a banner year in 1969, scoring two big hits, starting with "Traces," written by Cobb, Buie and studio bassist Emory Gordy Jr., which went to *Billboard*'s number-two position in March 1969. Buie and Cobb then borrowed an old gospel tune, "Every Day with Jesus," to create another hit, "Every Day with You, Girl." However, these were pretty much the last hits the Classics would score. The group would run on fumes for decades.

That same year, Walter Eaton was involved in a car crash, and his right leg was basically shattered. He was unable to walk for nearly a year. After a couple months in a hospital in Atlanta, Eaton went back to Jacksonville to recuperate, and there, he made the decision to stop touring. He figured it might be a good idea to build his own studio in Jacksonville. He had enough cachet—and gold records—to attract local musicians. This was during the period when the Second Coming became the Allman Brothers Band, and the music scene in Jacksonville was booming. The main problem with this plan was that most Jacksonville musicians didn't have money to pay for studio time. After two or three attempts to build new facilities—and racking up substantial losses—Eaton went out and got himself a steady job, again working for the city. The music biz was just too unpredictable and nerve-wracking, he said.[70]

The Classics continued to straggle along with various lineups led by Yost, but with Lowery's help, they landed a deal with Nashville-based MGM South, where Yost scored a couple minor hits. Yost continued touring with a reformed version of the Classics as the only original member.

Cobb and Buie launched the Atlanta Rhythm Section in 1970, which became quite successful. After leaving that group in 1987, Cobb moved to Nashville, where he worked at Chips Moman's Legends Studio. That's where he met and began working with the members of the supergroup the Highwaymen: Kris Kristofferson, Johnny Cash, Waylon Jennings and Willie Nelson.[71]

IN 1965, THE EMERALDS had three guitarists; Jimmy Amerson, J.R. Cobb and part-time member Jimmy Pitman. All three had been Paxon High students. Cobb left the Emeralds that year to join Walter Eaton's Classics. Amerson was later drafted, and that was the end of the Emeralds.

Pitman put together a trio with himself, bassist Mark Chamrey and drummer Jim McCormack. They headed to Daytona Beach to look for work.

Daytona, a favorite spot for tourists and spring breakers, was booming, music-wise. That same year, a group led by Seabreeze High School graduates Sylvan Wells and Pete Thomason cut a silly ditty called "Little Black Egg," recorded in a home studio and released on local label Lee Records. This record became legendary.

Local audio engineer Lee Hazen also made recordings of a Daytona group called the Escorts, led by guitar-playing siblings Duane and Gregg Allman. Duane Allman and Sylvan Wells had been classmates at Seabreeze. Wells recalled that in those early years Gregg Allman played lead while Duane played rhythm and did most of the singing.[72]

The Nightcrawlers was one of the few Daytona groups that performed a lot of original material, largely because, as Wells told an interviewer, its members weren't good enough to pick out the hits. Wells had never played guitar before forming the group.[73]

The Nightcrawlers' main competition was, of course, the Escorts, which would become the Allman Joys. Both groups were set to open for the Beach Boys at City Island Ball Park the day before Easter. It somehow occurred Wells that the group should write a paean to that holiday. Wells showed bassist Chuck Conlon the main riff and the chord progression, and Conlon wrote the lyrics and melody of what became "Little Black Egg."[74] The group performed it for the first time at the Beach Boys' show on April 17, 1965.

Without telling the band members, Hazen had taken a tape of a Nightcrawlers' song called "Cry" to a local station, WROD, which put it in rotation. The group scrambled to get some 45-rpm records pressed to meet the demand. The Nightcrawlers' follow-up single, "Little Black Egg," also got into rotation at WROD as well as other Florida stations. Soon, talent scouts from national labels started calling. Hy Grill of the New York–based Kapp Records (distributed by Decca) subsequently signed the group to a deal. The label sent the members to Criteria Recording in Miami to rerecord the song for nationwide distribution. The group eventually released three singles and one album through Kapp.[75]

The group's jangly style was categorized as "folk rock," which had been popularized by the Byrds in Los Angeles, the Beau Brummels in San Francisco and the Searchers in London; although, as a *Cash Box* reviewer pointed out, "Little Black Egg" sounds remarkably reminiscent of Buddy Holly and the Crickets.[76]

The Nightcrawlers' original lineup disbanded in 1966, with all five members going on to university. However, during the summer break that year, Wells and lead guitarist Thomason were back in Daytona. They figured there was still some quick cash to be made trading on the Nightcrawlers' name. The pair had heard Pitman's trio, the Nameless Ones.[77] Wells and Thomason offered to hire the three members to back them up in an ad hoc version of the Nightcrawlers. This arrangement lasted three months, but Pitman could then say he'd played with a national act.

By early 1967, "Little Black Egg" had broken through nationally, but the Nightcrawlers had dissolved. Still, the song lived on. Its success galvanized young rockers in the region, and the song's simple lead riff became a mandatory item in their repertoires. Over the years, it has been covered by perhaps thirty rock bands, but more importantly, it was the likely first song a generation of young guitarists learned on their instruments, primarily because it was so simple. That was its beauty. "It had to be easy, because I didn't know how to play much," Wells said.[78]

FOLK-ROCK DOMINATED THE LOS Angeles music scene in 1965. It started when the Byrds shot to number one with an electric version of Bob Dylan's "Mister Tambourine Man." Even a Jacksonville group jumped on the folk-rock bandwagon.

Scott Boyer had moved to the city from Binghamton, New York, with his family. His parents noted his musical aptitude and started taking him to piano lessons at the age of four. He took up the acoustic guitar after hearing Peter, Paul and Mary, whose version of "Blowin' in the Wind" led him to Dylan. He picked up the acoustic guitar, learned fingerpicking and became a "folkie." He also studied viola and violin, and after graduating from Englewood High School, where he played in the school orchestra, he continued his studies at Florida State University in Tallahassee.[79]

In the dorms, he ran into two former Englewood High graduates: David Brown, who played saxophone, and Claude "Butch" Trucks, who played drums and percussion and had already been in a Jacksonville band, the Vikings. Brown and Trucks had even jammed together back in Jacksonville. They heard the Byrds and decided to put together a folk-rock group. They knew Boyer and talked him into getting an electric twelve-string, and the Bitter End was born. To avoid any conflict with the Greenwich Village nightclub, they modified their name to "Bitter Ind."

They were so excited about their new band that they dropped out of school and headed to Daytona Beach to scout gigs. However, their style was not accepted there—you couldn't dance to it—so they reluctantly headed home. Back in Jacksonville, they landed a slot as the house band at the Comic

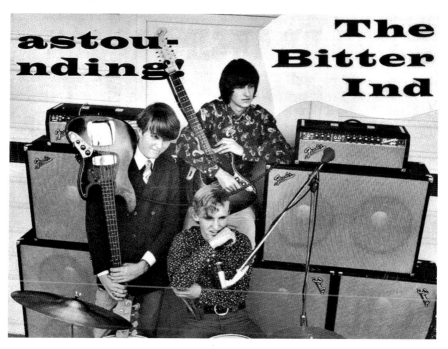

The Bitter Ind, circa 1966. *Left to right*: David Brown, Butch Trucks and Scott Boyer. *ACP Records publicity photograph.*

Book Club, thanks to a recommendation from Duane Allman, who had seen the group in Daytona.[80] This led to their obtaining a stint on a summer-replacement TV series called *Let's Go* on Channel Twelve (WFGA-TV).

The group became hugely popular and was taken on by talent manager Don Dana, who put out a single with his own ACP (Atlantic Coast Productions) label. He sent the group to Memphis to record, and they changed their name to Tiffany System. The group came up with a formulaic folk-rock rendition of Dylan's "It's All Over Now, Baby Blue" in cloying three-part harmony.[81] The trio also made a couple of singles for Minaret, a small Valparaiso, Florida label affiliated with Nashville executive Shelby Singleton, to no acclaim.

The group played all over the region, including at a 1968 Young Republican convention in Miami, where it attracted the attention of record distributor Henry Stone, along with producers Steve Alaimo and Brad Shapiro. Stone helped the group, now renamed the 31st of February, land a deal with New York–based folk (and folk-rock) label Vanguard Records.

Alaimo and Shapiro produced—on spec—a second album, which included prospective members Duane and Gregg Allman, along with the original recording of Gregg Allman's song "Melissa," but Vanguard declined its option to release a follow-up album.[82] At this point, the group members went their separate ways. Gregg Allman returned to Los Angeles to pick up the pieces of his recording deal with Liberty Records (under the name Hour Glass). Duane Allman moved to Jacksonville briefly before leaving for Muscle Shoals. Butch Trucks worked on some sessions as a member of Stone's studio band, the Zoo, as did Brown. Trucks soon returned to Jacksonville, intending to become a schoolteacher, while Brown remained in Miami doing session work. Scott Boyer moved to Gainesville, where he put together a working folk duo with Jacksonville musician Bill Pillmore, who had also attended Florida State University.

Boyer and Pillmore were thinking about putting a real band together when a friend from Orlando suggested they meet with guitarist-singer-songwriter Tommy Talton, who had been with the RCA Records act We the People and was available. Boyer and Talton hit it off right away. The parties involved decided to head for Jacksonville, where gigs were plentiful and the rents were low. There, they formed a group called Cowboy.[83]

One day, Duane Allman, on his way to Macon, stopped by Cowboy House near Riverside. Allman had already been signed by Phil Walden, and Butch Trucks was in his new band. Walden was in the process of forming Capricorn Records (distributed by Atco/Atlantic) and was

Cowboy en route to Martha's Vinyard, circa 1970. *Photograph by Chris Thibaut; used with permission.*

scouting new acts. Allman recommended Cowboy, and a deal was struck. After getting signed, the group members relocated to a farmhouse outside Macon, Walden's home base. Cowboy's first album release, *Reach for the Sky*, came out on Atco in 1970 and quickly fell off the face of the Earth. Obviously, the label did not have high hopes for the group, as only five thousand copies were pressed.[84]

Cowboy's style was much closer to West Coast country-rock than it was to what later became known as southern rock. "We were more California country-rock or maybe folk-rock," Talton said in an interview.[85] Cowboy sounded a lot like Poco or the Flying Burrito Brothers. Boyer said he had been following Gram Parsons's career since his Jacksonville days. Talton, too, was a fan of Parsons.[86]

Boyer and Talton eventually decided they needed a new band, and a purge was implemented.[87] In the meantime, the pair landed a gig as backup musicians in Gregg Allman's 1974 solo band. David Brown, Boyer's old cohort from the Bitter Ind, played tenor saxophone in this outfit.

That same year, Eric Clapton recorded one of Boyer's songs, "Please Be with Me," a laconic country-rock ballad from Cowboy's second album, on which Duane Allman had added a Dobro. All this generated enough

41

Cowboy, circa 1976. *Left to right*: David Brown, Scott Boyer, Bill Stewart, Randall Bramblett and Tommy Talton. *Capricorn Records publicity photograph.*

interest to keep Cowboy going, despite its lack of sales. In 1976, Brown, who had been playing bass with with Boz Scaggs—a gig Duane Allman had recommended him for—came to Macon to join Cowboy. This lineup did not last long, however. The group's 1977 album, *Cowboy*, would be its last for Capricorn.

Boyer moved to Los Angeles to pursue a songwriting career. Then he moved to northern Alabama, where he worked with several bands, a couple of which included Talton. He recorded a solo album in Muscle Shoals, *All My Friends*, in 1991. The pair staged a Cowboy reunion in 2010, but they were the only original members, with the exception of Bill Pillmore, who played steel guitar on two songs.[88]

Boyer continued to record sporadically in varying configurations. He died in 2018, due to complications from peripheral artery disease. Talton now lives in Atlanta, where he continues to record and write songs. He told an interviewer, "No one could write a more beautiful ballad than Scott Boyer."[89]

HAVING HAD A TASTE of the big-time with the Nightcrawlers, Jimmy Pitman decided to head for the bright lights of Los Angeles. This was a rather unusual—and bold—move, since most Jacksonville musicians went to either Miami or Atlanta, both only a five-hour drive, in search of fame and fortune. Los Angeles is 2,400 miles from Jacksonville, more or less a three-day drive. In the 1960s, Los Angeles was burgeoning as the new mecca for pop music, but the competition was fierce. You had to know someone. You couldn't just come in off the street.

Pitman had somehow met Murry Wilson, the father of the Wilson siblings, at a Beach Boys show. Wilson suggested Pitman might make it in Los Angeles, so Pitman took the trip, hoping Wilson could hook him up somehow.[90]

Once he was ensconced in Hollywood, Pitman joined a group called the Happy Apples, which was managed by a local promoter. Jacksonville drummer Jim McCormack also happened to be in Hollywood, so Pitman brought him on board. Pitman was interviewed in a 1968 documentary for NBC-TV called *Experiment in Television* as one of several spokespersons for American youth and their music. However, the group's manager was unable to land a recording contract, and the group broke up soon after.[91]

Pitman was in the right place at the right time. Psychedelia was lighting up the music world. A group from Glendale called the Strawberry Alarm Clock (SAC) had scored a number-one hit in November 1967 with "Incense and Peppermints." However, by the time Pitman was recruited as the group's new lead singer and guitarist, SAC was in the process of disintegrating. The group's label, Uni Records (a division of MCA), was contractually

Left: Jimmy Pitman with Strawberry Alarm Clock (*fourth from left in front of Ed King*), 1969. *Right*: Pitman with Jumbo (*third from the left in front*), 1970. *Publicity photographs.*

committed to another album, so the members decided to regroup and give it one last shot.

Pitman was brought in as SAC's new frontman, as well as its lead guitarist. Virtuoso guitarist Ed King, who would later move to Jacksonville as a member of Lynyrd Skynyrd, switched to bass. Pitman joined just in time to work on SAC's third album, *Good Morning Starshine*, which was released in May 1969. He cowrote most of the songs on the album and wrote three by himself, which took the group in a new, heavier direction (with the exception of its gloopy title track, a truly terrible rendition of a silly song from the musical *Hair* with a bloated vocal arrangement that sounds like the Association). The album turned out to be a spotty affair that confused fans and critics alike. Reviewer Lindsay Planer, in *AllMusic*, calls the album "the antithesis of what the band had been."[92] Nor did it bother the charts. SAC was starting to buckle under the strain of legal and personnel problems, with former members filing writs. Pitman abandoned the sinking ship just two months after the album's release.

During his time in Hollywood, Pitman again ran into Duane and Gregg Allman, whose new group, Hour Glass, had been signed to Los Angeles–based Liberty Records. Pitman hung out and jammed with the Daytona boys, who seemed destined for greatness.

He landed another lucky break with a new group called Jumbo. Things looked promising as Jumbo signed with Lou Adler's Ode Records (home of the soon-to-be-multiplatinum-selling Carole King). In 1970, the group released a single, "Not So Bad," which incorporated style elements from Steppenwolf, Grand Funk Railroad and Chicago; again, success was not in the cards.

Pitman packed his stuff and headed back to Florida. He was a favorite among musicians in Jacksonville because he was not only talented but also affable. "Jimmy was always one of the coolest guys," Jacksonville guitarist and bassist Rick NesSmith said. "He was born cool."[93]

In the early 1980s, Pitman moved to Salt Lake City to work with a short-lived group called Thunderchicken. While he was there, he decided to put together a new version of SAC, featuring himself.[94] This group toured the West for a few years until it ran out of steam. Pitman again found himself in Jacksonville. Tired of scuffling, he gave up music as a full-time pursuit but continued playing in various local groups, none of which ever scratched the big-time.

Pitman's old friend Jimmy Amerson described his playing as simple but effective. Pitman was limited to pentatonic scales, Amerson said, but he was very rhythmic. "He didn't overplay and was good at playing something that grooved with the rhythm section," Amerson said. "I think all this came from the fact that he was the lead singer. He had a good stage presence and charisma."[95]

THE BIGGEST THING SINCE
THE VENTURES

*T*he Beatles came to Jacksonville in September 1964, the day after Hurricane Dora hit, leaving hundreds of budding young guitar players in their wake. There is no need to go into detail about the group here, but suffice it to say the Beatles were the inspiration for thousands of wannabe guitarists and rockstars all over the western world. Jacksonville was no exception; in fact, the city may have been more affected than most, as it was one of the group's few tour stops in the South. Of course, the Beatles had already made their initial splash on the *Ed Sullivan Show* in February.

When Lake Shore Junior High School (now Lake Shore Middle School) student Rick Doeschler saw the Beatles at Jacksonville's Gator Bowl, he knew what he had to do with his life. "Seeing them on *Ed Sullivan* was the deal," he said. "Seeing them [live, in person] was the icing on the cake. I was completely hooked."[96]

Doeschler, whose family lived in the idyllic Ortega Forest subdivision and was not musical, had never thought about playing an instrument. "I didn't know anybody who played guitar." His mother got him a cheap Harmony acoustic at Al's Pawn Shop downtown. He took a few lessons from a local folksinger who was big on the Kingston Trio. The first song Doeschler learned was "Greenback Dollar" (which was written by former Jacksonville resident Hoyt Axton). Doeschler told his teacher he preferred to learn the Beatles' music, but "he wasn't into the Beatles at all."

Doeschler desperately wanted an electric guitar. He hinted to his parents that this might make a good Christmas present, so his mother took him to

Left: Rick Doeschler with his Gretsch Tennessean, 1966. *Photograph by Marla Harris Middlecome; used with permission. Right*: Doeschler with the same guitar in 2022. *Photograph by the author*.

Paulus Music downtown. He had hoped for a Gretsch Country Gentleman, like the one George Harrison played (already made famous by Chet Atkins), but the price was too steep, so he settled for a Tennessean. He also picked up a used Gibson amplifier.[97]

Soon, Doeschler was in hog heaven, learning Beatles tunes along with "Little Black Egg" (of course), "Gloria" and "It's All Over Now." Doeschler and his guitarist friend Taylor Corse, who also sang, were never interested in instrumentals, he said, so they skipped the Ventures. This was a new era.

In early 1965, Doeschler and Corse, who lived in Venetia, just south of Ortega, put together a little combo called the Squires with the standard lineup of two guitars, a bass and drums. Corse sang all the songs until a Lake Shore resident and neighborhood tough named Ronnie Van Zant came along a year or so later.

Another Westside guitar nut, Allen Collins, lived across the Cedar River in nearby Cedar Hills, a typical cinderblock neighborhood like so many that sprang up in the 1950s and 1960s. Until this point, Collins had wanted to be a racecar driver.[98] After witnessing the Beatles on the *Ed Sullivan Show*, Collins and his best friend since kindergarten, bassist Larry Steele, put together a little group they called the Mods. Collins focused on rhythm guitar, so he brought in neighborhood hotshot Donnie Ulsh, who had been giving Collins some informal lessons, on lead guitar. Steele wrote:

That afternoon, we all met up at [drummer James Rice's] *house. By dark, we had decided we'd call ourselves the Mods, after the well-dressed, musical subculture in England we had read about in Tiger Beat magazine….We would also have a repertoire of three songs, "Louie Louie," "Wipeout" and "Green Onions."…It was 1964, and our little group of twelve-year-olds was out to conquer the world.*[99]

It was imperative for young players to own quality instruments if they expected to be taken seriously.[100] Collins, whose mother indulged him when it came to expensive guitars, had a new Gibson Melody Maker, which he got from Paulus Music, and a tiny Truetone amplifier. Ulsh had a very expensive Gibson ES-335 and a Gibson Invader amplifier. Steele was sheepish about his Japanese-made Kent bass. The Mods started leaning more toward the grittier British groups like the Rolling Stones and the Animals. However, after they heard the Byrds' version of Bob Dylan's "Mister Tambourine Man," they switched gears and began learning as many Byrds tunes as they could.[101]

With no gigs forthcoming, the boys would go out on Saturday nights to educate themselves on their new careers. They frequented various teen centers—there were plenty of those—and got inspired by other experienced local bands. One of their favorites was the Dalton Gang, which Steele calls "the finest band in the Southeast at the time." That group featured local guitar phenomenon Auburn Burrell, who would go on to become a well-known studio musician (see chapter 2). Their other local favorites were the Vikings, along with Tiny and the Surfers, both from the Northside.[102]

The Mods finally landed a few gigs at some Westside teen clubs, as well as a New Year's Eve party at the Springfield Lions Club. Steele recounted:

[W]*e were surprised to learn that we were not the only band in Lakeshore Junior High after all. Word had it that there was a new band called the Squires who were supposedly really good. These guys were a year older than us, and three of the four were Ortegans.*[103]

Taylor Corse, the rhythm guitarist for the Squires, filled in for Donnie Ulsh at the Mods' New Year's gig but had not mentioned the fact that he had his own group.

It was time for a showdown.

It was 3:00 p.m. in the school cafeteria, but it felt like high noon in Dodge City. The cafeteria was packed with sweaty students and a few teachers.

The Mods, New Year's Eve, 1966. *Left to right*: James Rice, Larry Steele, Allen Collins and Taylor Corse (filling in for Donnie Ulsh). *From the book* As I Recall, *by Larry Steele; courtesy of Theresa Askins Steele.*

Someone at Lake Shore Junior High School had organized a "battle of the bands," pitting the Mods against the Squires. There would be no prize or reward—only bragging rights.

The Mods were up first, ready to rumble in their light-blue Gant shirts and blue "cord" slacks. Ulsh did the singing for the group, except for some background vocals that were done by Collins and Steele. Their set list was predictable: Beatles, Rolling Stones, Animals, Byrds. The audience dutifully cheered after every number. The group closed with the Animals' "House of the Rising Sun," sans organ.[104]

A brief intermission ensued, and on came the Squires in their white turtleneck pullovers under navy-blue blazers and carefully styled Beatles-like haircuts. Guitarists Rick Doeschler and Taylor Corse sported matching jumbo-bodied Gretsch Tennessean guitars that looked almost as big as they were. Their repertoire almost exactly matched that of the Mods.[105] Again, the audience cheered wildly.

The judges determined the Mods had won. Adversaries Steele and Doeschler have both insisted it was a toss-up.[106] Judges decided a rematch was in order. A new battle was arranged and then moved to a larger facility, the gymnasium at nearby J.E.B. Stuart Middle School, scheduled for May 27. Van Zant, now a member of the Squires—which he renamed Us—decided his group would go on last. Van Zant exhibited none of the bullying behavior he became notorious for in Lynyrd Skynyrd. Van Zant took charge of the group, but "he was soft-spoken and polite," Doeschler said. "He was older, so we looked up to him."[107]

The Mods, in preparation, had coaxed respected guitarist Jerry Zambito from local group 4+1 to provide some pointers on their presentation; Zambito even lent Donnie Ulsh his Fender Vibrolux amplifier.[108] "The gym was packed to the rafters," Steele recounted, "and electricity was in the air by the time the Mods took the stage." He recalled his group performing flawlessly.

When it was time for Us to take the stage, guitarist Taylor Corse's Gibson amplifier would not come on. Allen Collins graciously offered to let him use his new Fender Super Reverb. Us played flawlessly as well, closing with a Beach Boys hit, "Sloop John B," which, by Steele's estimation, brought the house down. He also credits Van Zant's stage presence with being a winning factor in Us's victory.[109]

In 1966, Gary Rossington, another Lake Shore Junior High School student, got bit by the guitar bug. His mother helped him acquire a Gibson Firebird and a Fender amplifier, and he started getting together with Allen Collins—already a professional—to share pointers.[110]

Rossington, who lived on the other side of Cassatt Avenue, inside the city limits, had been hanging out with fellow Lake Shore student Bob Burns, who lived in Hyde Park. He told interviewer Lee Ballinger:

> I decided I'd get a paper route and start collecting Coke bottles, and I bought a guitar from Sears and Roebuck. It was a Silvertone. It came [with an amplifier] in the case….I bought that for sixty bucks, I think. It seems like it took me five years to pay for it.[111]

Bob Burns said in a filmed interview that it was his idea to form a group. He invited bassist Larry Junstrom, who lived only a couple blocks from the Burns household in the same subdivision. "First, it was me and Larry." They needed a guitarist. Burns knew just the guy: Gary Rossington, who lived about a mile away. The three were christened Me, You and Him.[112]

Meanwhile, Us guitarists Rick Doeschler and Taylor Corse transferred to Lee High. They decided they had other things they wanted to do with their

Carport in Westside's Hyde Park District, where Gary Rossington and Bob Burns first jammed in 1966. *Photograph by the author.*

free time, like play tennis and go out with girls. They both knew it would only be a matter of time before they had to get real jobs. Unlike Rossington and Collins, they realized that trying to make it big in the music business was probably just a pipe dream, and they were not prepared to gamble everything on it. The pair quit, and the band fell apart.

Us singer Ronnie Van Zant, however, wanted to keep going. He'd heard about Burns's new group and showed up unannounced at his house. Burns recalled:

> *The way I met Ronnie: he knocked on my door one morning, right before school. I said, "I don't wanna fight you, man." And he said, "I ain't here to fight." He says, "I'm a singer, man." I said, "You're a singer?" He said, "Yeah." I said, "I'll be dang." I said, "I got a bass player, and I have a guitar player. Why don't let's try to put something together."* [113]

Deciding they needed another guitarist—someone with an amp—Burns suggested Allen Collins, who had a nice Fender. The three went around the neighborhood looking for him. They found him pedaling his bicycle home from school.

51

Their timing proved to be perfect. Larry Steele wrote that Collins had been upset with him for hurting him in what was supposed to be a good-natured wrestling match that got out of hand. Collins was therefore eager to leave the Mods, but members of the Mods objected; Donnie Ulsh got Collins on the phone and unwisely threatened him with bodily harm if he didn't come back. This was the exact wrong tack, Steele said: Collins's feeling of being physically menaced was likely the reason he left the group in the first place.[114]

Ronnie Van Zant and his neighborhood friend (later bodyguard) Gene Odom, who was even tougher, went over to James Rice's house, where Rice, Steele and Ulsh were gathered. It was amicably agreed that Collins would join the new group without any interference from his former bandmates and that no further discussion was called for.[115]

Van Zant asked Rick Doeschler if he would help Collins and Rossington learn some tunes Us had performed, which Van Zant hoped to sing in the new group. The three went over to the Doeschler home in Ortega to study. Doeschler's father, Rick said, was a bit leery of these shady-looking Westsiders. "Keep an eye on the silverware," Rick's father told his mother.[116]

With four members, the new group dropped the moniker Me, You and Him. The unnamed group had a gig booked at St. Matthews Church's fall festival, but by this point, Junstrom had gone off with a working group called After Five. A third guitarist, Billy Skaggs, was brought in to fill out the sound.[117] Perhaps this was the genesis of the "three-guitar army." The group would soon adopt the name the Pretty Ones.[118] After that, they became the Noble Five, One Percent, Leonard Skinner and finally Lynyrd Skynyrd.[119]

IT WAS AROUND THE time of the battles of the bands that Dave Hlubek's family moved back to Jacksonville. Hlubek, the son of a sailor, had been born in Jacksonville, but his father had been transferred to the West Coast (and Hawaii) when he was a child. After a divorce, his mother returned to her hometown, where she later remarried, and Hlubek transferred to Lake Shore Junior High.[120]

Steele wrote that when Hlubek arrived at the school in 1966, he claimed to be a former rhythm guitarist for the Doors. That group had yet to release a record but was already getting coverage in teen magazines. Steele recalled meeting Hlubek between classes: "I couldn't wait to meet the guy who had

Lake Shore Middle School, formerly Lake Shore Junior High. *Photograph by the author.*

the balls to create such an unbelievable backstory and had already gained a number of fans around school as a result."

> "Hey, man, aren't you David?" I asked.
> "Yeah, I'm David," he answered.
> "I hear you were the rhythm guitarist for the Doors," I said....
> "That's right! How ya doin', man?" he quipped, extending his hand with a big smile.
> "Well, the Doors don't even have a bass player, much less a rhythm guitar player," I laughed.
> "Well, duh! That's because I moved to Jacksonville," David said, flashing another big smile. With that, Hlubek turned and walked away. I was dumbfounded.[121]

4

FLORIDA'S KINGPINS

Psychedelia arrived in Florida in 1968 on a wave of Orange Sunshine. That was the year the Blues Messengers, led by Bradenton guitarist Dickey Betts, moved to Jacksonville. At that point, the music, later dubbed "acid-rock," was referred to as "underground."

"Dickey Betts was the hottest guitar player in the area," keyboardist Reese Wynans told Alan Paul. "[He was] the guy everyone looked up to and wanted to emulate."[122]

Inspired by the new movement emanating from California and England, Betts and bassist Berry Oakley (formerly with Tommy Roe's backing group, the Roemans) decided to surf the psychedelic wave. Their group, the Blues Messengers, was spotted at a Tampa bar by Jacksonville nightclub owner Leonard Renzler, who co-owned several juke joints, including the R&R Bar downtown and Westside's Golden Gate Lounge (where the Classics had been the house band; see chapter 2).

Betts had been coming to Jacksonville since the mid-1960s, when he led the house band at Westside's Normandy Club with his group the Jesters. He told his friend and former bandmate Mack Doss, formerly of Bradenton's Thunderbeats (a group that also included guitar sensation Larry "Rhino" Reinhardt) that if he wanted regular work as a guitarist, Jacksonville was the place to be. Doss packed his gear and headed on up.[123]

Betts was reluctant to abandon the top-forty repertoire that kept bread on his table, but he put his faith in Oakley's instincts. The Second Coming, consisting of Betts; Oakley; Betts's wife, Dale; and drummer John Meeks,

Mack Doss (*left*) with Dickey Betts, circa 2005. *Photograph by Gail Grimm Gerdes, BOSK Photograph; used with permission.*

arrived in April 1968 and began working six nights a week at the new club on Roosevelt Boulevard called the Scene, quickly becoming the most prominent rock group in town. "We were the only [guys] in town with long hair," Betts told interviewer Andy Aledort of *Vintage Guitar*. "We'd be driving around, and people would throw shit at us."[124]

Duane and Gregg Allman came up from Daytona Beach a couple of times to sit in with the Second Coming at the Scene. Betts had met Duane Allman on the circuit in the mid-1960s, but the two did not hit it off.[125] But Allman became a fan of Betts—and vice versa.

One of Betts's major influences was Cream's Eric Clapton. In fact, Clapton, who had made a name for himself in London with the Yardbirds in the mid-1960s, would become a major influence for many, if not most, players in the region, including Allen Collins, Dave Hlubek and Don Barnes. Betts used to perform a version of "Crossroads" that was very similar to Cream's; he also performed Cream's "I Feel Free," which the Second Coming released as a single with New Jersey–based Steady Records.[126]

Dale Betts got pregnant during the group's stint in Jacksonville, so keyboardist Reese Wynans came up from Sarasota to fill in for her. After Dale had her baby, she moved out front, and Wynans remained on keyboards. At first, the group had two guitarists, but not long after arriving in Jacksonville, second guitarist Larry Reinhardt split to form his own power trio called the Load. Wynans told an interviewer:

> *The Second Coming played six nights a week at the Scene. Our repertoire was about half rock and half blues. Dickey played most of the blues, and Larry Reinhardt did most of the rock....Dickey sang* [numbers like] *"Born in Chicago" and "Born under a Bad Sign." Larry Reinhardt did a bunch of Hendrix covers....Dale sang some Jefferson Airplane.* [127]

The Load, who included bassist Richard Price and drummer Monty Young, went to work at Dub's Steer Room in nearby Gainesville. Reinhardt, a stunning player, would go on to fame and (a bit of) fortune with Iron Butterfly and, later, Wynans in Captain Beyond. Probably none of what he did could be called "southern rock."

The Second Coming hired a manager, Allen Facemire, who hosted his own Sunday-night radio program called the *Underground Circus* on WAPE-AM. He was in tune with the band and their music and understood what they hoped to accomplish. Facemire played the Second Coming's Steady single on his show.

The Second Coming was working six nights a week at the Scene but became frustrated when the local hippies—most of whom were too young to get into bars—didn't show up, and they found themselves playing for mostly sailors. Oakley felt the group's true audience was out there; they just had to find a way to reach them. He came up with the idea of playing for free in the parks on Sundays, the group's only day off. These free concerts, based on similar gatherings in San Francisco, were called "be-ins." Before long, other underground acts joined in, and these jams set Jacksonville's youth music scene on fire. Musicians like Duane Allman, Butch Trucks, Donn Finney (formerly of Tiny and the Surfers and later with Wet Willie) would come from all over northeast Florida to jam.

The be-ins were held in various locations, such as the Forrest Inn on the Westside, Greenfield Stables out toward Atlantic Beach and other areas, but the favored spot was Riverside's Willowbranch Park. One of the groups that often played in the park was called Wapaho Aspirin Company, led by siblings Dave and Gary Goddard on lead guitar and bass, respectively. Gary Goddard, probably the best singer in town at that time, later formed a guitar-less trio, with Reese Wynans on keyboard and Fuzzy Land on drums, called

Ugly Jellyroll, who performed at the Forrest Inn. Goddard was the singer in that group as well. Aspiring singer Ronnie Van Zant told Randall Hall that Goddard was "the best [singer] in the business."[128]

The Forrest Inn was the site of some very important Sunday afternoon be-ins. When Duane Allman came to town to secretly audition players for his new band—which would become the Allman Brothers Band—he led a jam session or two there. Berry Oakley, whom Allman had already decided to include in his band on bass, participated, as did Betts and drummers Butch Trucks and Jaimoe (also known as Johnny Johnson from Mississippi, whom Allman had brought down from Macon). Saxophonist Donn Finney also participated in these jams, which were captured on film by former Lee High student McGregor McGehee.

LIKE MOST ELECTRIC GUITARISTS of this era, Duane and Gregg Allman started out playing the Ventures and surf music.[129] Gregg was the one who first took up the guitar; like so many others, his first guitar was a Silvertone, which he bought at Sears with the money he earned from a paper route.[130] After getting himself a Fender Musicmaster, Gregg played lead while Duane played rhythm and did most of the singing in their first group, the Shufflers.[131]

Before forming their own groups, the brothers worked with Bob Greenlee's R&B band the House Rockers, who played regularly at the Daytona Beach Pier.[132] Duane Allman credited House Rockers guitarist Jim Shepley with being his primary inspiration for taking up the guitar professionally.[133] Another important influence on Duane's playing was Lonnie Mack, whose 1963 version of "Memphis" Duane had mastered while in military school.[134]

The brothers' second group was the Escorts, which morphed into the Allman Joys. That group landed some prime gigs through a couple of well-connected booking agencies in Atlanta and Nashville, playing as far afield as New York's Greenwich Village and St. Louis's Gaslight Square.

While performing at Nashville's Briar Patch, the Allman Joys were spotted by songwriter-producer John D. Loudermilk, who took them to Buddy Killen's Dial Records (distributed by Atlantic), where the group released one single, a remake of Howlin' Wolf's "Spoonful." The record deal was a big break for the boys, but it went nowhere. An album's worth of material was recorded at Bradley's Barn but was not released until many years later.[135]

The Allman Joys, circa 1965. Gregg Allman (*top left*) and Duane Allman (*top right*).
Publicity photograph.

The brothers had performed several times in Jacksonville as the Allman Joys as well as in a later incarnation called Hour Glass, which had been signed to Liberty Records in 1967 and was based in Los Angeles.

Ronnie Van Zant had idolized Gregg Allman ever since he first heard Hour Glass's debut album. His group One Percent happened to be the house band at the Comic Book when Hour Glass arrived on July 12, 1968. One Percent served as the opening act. Incredible as it seems, One Percent played Hour Glass's entire debut album, after which Hour Glass got up and played the same songs.[136]

Disheartened by their lack of recognition and record sales, the members of Hour Glass went their separate ways. Duane Allman knew Jacksonville drummer Butch Trucks, who had once subbed for the Allman Joys' drummer at the Comic Book. Trucks's popular folk-rock group, the 31st of February (formerly the Bitter Ind), was hoping to get Vanguard Records to release another album and decided to expand the trio to a quintet with the addition of Duane and Gregg Allman. The expanded lineup made an album's worth of demos at Criteria in Miami with producers Steve Alaimo and Brad Shapiro, but Vanguard declined to release the material.

Gregg Allman decided to move back to Los Angeles in an unsuccessful bid to resuscitate Hour Glass with Los Angeles session musicians, now called Gregg Allman and Hour Glass.

DUANE ALLMAN DECIDED TO move to Jacksonville. He hung out with the members of the Second Coming and even moved into the house where three of them lived. The "Gray House" on 2844 Riverside Avenue had been carved up into tiny apartments. After staying with the Oakleys for a spell, Allman moved into the bottom apartment with artist Ellen Hopkins.[137] He participated in several jam sessions with the Second Coming. The following is an excerpt from a letter Allman wrote to his girlfriend Donna Roosman in St. Louis:

> [There have been] *these huge gatherings of freaks* [hippies] *in Jacksonville, Florida, every Sunday for the past few weeks. Millions of bands play, and it's really fun; I wish you could be here to see it—it's a miracle....I've been living there for quite a while with friends, and I'll probably stay until* [I] *move to Muscle Shoals.*[138]

"Gray House" at 2844 Riverside Avenue. *Photograph by the author.*

It is not unreasonable to speculate that Allman was angling to join the Second Coming. When this didn't happen, he decided to bolt to Muscle Shoals, home of Rick Hall's Florence, Alabama Music Enterprises, where he had recorded with Hour Glass, to try to become a session player.[139] Allman happened to know Alabama guitarist Eddie Hinton, who was born in Jacksonville, Florida, but raised in Tuscaloosa, a couple of hours' drive from Florence.[140] Hinton was serving in FAME's house band and let Allman crash in his living room for a while.[141]

Allman's trip to Muscle Shoals turned out to be a very lucky roll of the dice. Rick Hall was wary of Allman: "He had long, white hair and looked like a junkie."[142] Not only did Allman eventually win Hall over with his playing—and his musical ideas—Hall put him on sessions with soul giants Clarence Carter, Wilson Pickett and Aretha Franklin. Atlantic Records' vice-president Jerry Wexler was bowled over when he heard Allman's extended guitar solo on Pickett's version of "Hey, Jude." Wexler summoned Allman, along with the rest of the Muscle Shoals Rhythm Section, to New York to play on Franklin's next album.

Allman's stock soared, and so did he. There were problems, however. Allman didn't write and was a weak singer. Allman brought Oakley up from Jacksonville a few times and also brought in former Hour Glass members

Johnny Sandlin on drums and Paul Hornsby on keyboards (both lived in Alabama). Hall was not satisfied with the results—and, he said, he got tired of the group's lackadaisical work ethic—so he decided to get rid of them. He sold Allman's contract to Wexler at Atlantic. Wexler said, "I loved his playing so much, I bought his contract from Hall for $15,000."[143]

So, Allman had a record deal but still no band. Wexler decided to bring Macon talent manager Phil Walden on board to help Allman put together a full-time group.[144]

Even with a major label deal in the works, bassist Oakley remained dubious about leaving the Second Coming. Allman went back to Jacksonville with drummer Johnson in tow to try to convince him to come on board. They landed at drummer Butch Trucks's house in the Arlington section. Trucks was brought in as a second drummer. They then went over to the Gray House in Riverside to grab Oakley. Several jam sessions ensued, including one at the Forrest Inn (see the photograph below). Oakley was still reluctant to leave Betts in the lurch, since forming the Second Coming had been his idea. Allman was impressed with Betts's playing. "Eric Clapton's got nothing on Dickey Betts," he said.[145] Allman decided Betts would be an asset to his group, and the lineup was near complete. This dual guitar attack, with both players alternating on lead as well as playing duets, would become the group's secret weapon.

Duane Allman leading a jam session at Westside's Forrest Inn, 1969. Note the dual-drummer configuration is already in place. *Photograph by Charles Faubion; used with permission.*

Needing a singer, Duane called his brother in Los Angeles and told him to get his butt back to Florida—he now had a record deal with a major label and complete creative control.[146] Within three days, Gregg Allman appeared at the Gray House, where he started writing songs for the group, including "Whipping Post" and "Black Hearted Woman," which would appear on the group's first Atco album.[147]

A couple of youngsters from a Westside group called One Percent dropped in at the Gray House one afternoon and asked Gregg for advice on how to write songs.[148] Gary Rossington told interviewer Arlene Weiss:

We went to see the Allman Brothers, but they were called the Allman Joys back then. We loved them, and I remember two or three times we saw them. We got to know Gregg, and we asked them how they wrote songs....And they said, "We just sit down on a floor, and we don't get up until it's written."[149]

The new group played two shows—the first on March 29 at the Beaches Auditorium and the second on March 30 at the Cedar Hills National Guard Armory—with the Second Coming and the Load. The Load opened, the Second Coming was up next and the show culminated in a massive jam session with members from both groups, along with Duane Allman. Gregg was in attendance at both gigs but did not perform because Reese Wynans already had the keyboards covered, and there hadn't been time to rehearse with Gregg.[150]

With the new lineup intact, Walden summoned the still-unnamed band to Macon. The group left town on April Fools' Day 1968.

———— ⌘ ————

MUCH HAS BEEN WRITTEN about Duane Allman's playing but not enough about Betts's.

The Allman Brothers Band was essentially a psychedelic blues and soul band with elements of jazz tossed in. Betts, however, had been raised on bluegrass and country; he played mandolin in a bluegrass band when he was a youngster.[151] Betts started out on ukulele before taking up the mandolin. He got bit by the electric guitar bug at the age of sixteen after hearing Duane Eddy. Chuck Berry was also a major inspiration for him.[152]

Although he had become a Clapton acolyte by the time he moved to Jacksonville with the Second Coming, Betts managed to outgrow that, creating an original style that revolutionized southern rock and more. Andy Aledort of *Guitar World* wrote, "[Betts] possesses one of the most distinct and influential guitar styles in the history of rock."[153]

Playing major pentatonic scales—basically country-type licks—over blues was nothing new; Eric Clapton had done it, as had Albert King, B.B. King and others, but Betts, possibly encouraged by the West Coast country-rock movement, started leaning toward more of a bluegrass than a blues feel. The first piece on which Betts deployed this style was "Mountain Jam" (which was based on a motif from Donovan's "There Is a Mountain"), released on

ABB's 1972 Capricorn Records album, *Eat a Peach*. However, the band had been performing this rambling jam onstage since its inception.

Betts was certainly not the first electric guitarist to bring a bluegrass feel to rock music. There had been several West Coast players in the country-rock field attempting to merge bluegrass with rock, such as Clarence White of the Byrds, Bernie Leadon of the Flying Burrito Brothers and the Eagles and Jerry Garcia of the Grateful Dead—all of whom, like Betts, had bluegrass backgrounds.

Jacksonville guitarist Steve Wheeler speculates that Betts's transformation was necessary in order for Betts to create a style that was distinct from Duane Allman's.[154] He described Betts's approach as evincing a pronounced fluidity, unlike straight blues, which is rather choppy and generally contains a lot of rests. Plus, Betts's touch—like Clapton's—is supple rather than forceful. Allman, on the other hand, wielded a style that was cutting and aggressive—angry as a hornet. Aside from his elegant picking style, Betts added a continual flow of eighth notes, as if his fingers were dancing on the fretboard, which was a common aspect of bluegrass flatpicking, as well as mandolin playing.[155] There was also a touch of Django Reinhardt in Betts's style.[156]

Betts took the Clapton—and the jazz—approach, picking notes lightly, using a Gibson paired with a Marshall amplifier. He brought Clapton's touch and tone to country music. Of course, this wasn't exactly country anymore—it was country-rock.

In the early 1970s, as the West Coast country-rock movement gained traction, Betts tried his hand at it as a songwriter and singer.[157] First, he came up with "Blue Sky," which appeared on *Eat a Peach*. This country-rock venture constituted a decidedly anomalous direction for the group. "Blue Sky" foreshadowed Betts's next country-rock outing, "Ramblin' Man," which appeared on the ABB's 1973 album, *Brothers and Sisters*.

It happened that Betts's country influences were timely. With the Eagles' "Take It Easy" preceding it by seven months, "Ramblin' Man," featuring Betts on lead vocals, was released as a single and—to the band members' surprise—soared to the number-two spot on *Billboard's* pop chart. It was the group's only top-forty hit. Drummer Butch Trucks told ABB biographer Alan Paul, "We all thought 'Ramblin' Man' was too country to even record. It was a good song, but it didn't sound like us."[158]

In 1974, Betts recorded his first solo album, *Highway Call*, which included bluegrass great Vassar Clements on fiddle. A couple years later, when the ABB broke up (for the first time), Betts put together his own band, Great

Southern, which focused on his fusion of rock, blues, country, bluegrass and jazz.

Betts is now retired, living near the Highway 41 he sang about in "Ramblin' Man," but he should be remembered for creating a style that was very influential, echoes of which can be heard in players like Jeff Carlisi of 38 Special, Toy Caldwell of the Marshall Tucker Band, Barry Bailey of the Atlanta Rhythm Section and many more.[159]

Prominent Jacksonville guitarist Jim Graves, who moved to Jacksonville in 1972, said Betts was his guitar hero. He said, as with many Florida players, Clapton ignited his love affair with the electric guitar, but Betts took his interest to the next level.[160]

Steve Wheeler agreed: "Anybody who wanted to play southern rock was influenced by Betts. You had to have that style in your toolbox."[161]

Even Duane Allman said he thought Betts was a superior player. "I'm the famous guitar player," Allman told an interviewer, "but Dickey is the good one."[162]

5

SOUTHERN ROCKERS

*T*he local boys, such as Allen Collins, Gary Rossington and Dave Hlubek, found they had to step up their game after the Tampa Bay cats came to town. But within a year, those cats had up and gone, mostly to Macon, Georgia, 240 miles northwest of Jacksonville (about a four-hour trip by car).

Larry Reinhardt was hanging out in Macon, on the lookout for an opportunity, when someone from Iron Butterfly's management called manager Phil Walden's office, looking for a guitarist. Whoever it was called the right place. Reinhardt went out to Los Angeles, where he joined Butterfly—probably the first heavy-metal group—along with fellow Tampa-area guitarist Mike Pinera.

Dru Lombar was another Jacksonville musician who joined the exodus to Macon. Lombar was inspired to become a musician after seeing Elvis Presley perform, in this case, in the 1958 movie *King Creole*. "He was playing [an acoustic] guitar. I thought to myself, 'This is what I want to do.'"[163]

Like Westside guitarists Jimmy Amerson and Jimmy Pitman, Lombar had been knocked out by Freddie King's 1960 R&B instrumental "Hideaway."[164] Lombar soon became a fan of the blues and soul and a regular listener of Hoss Allen's nighttime show on WLAC-AM.[165] He started playing electric at the age of eleven, studying the work of Chuck Berry, Duane Eddy, Lonnie Mack and, of course, the Ventures.[166]

The first professional musicians Lombar met were members of the Jacksonville group the Echoes, whose drummer was Dennis Yost.[167] When the British Invasion came along in 1964, he was ready to rock.

Duncan U. Fletcher High School in Jacksonville Beach spawned a number of teen bands, said guitarist-vocalist Anthony Martinich, who attended the school in the late 1960s, along with Lombar. In 1964, the two formed teen group the Soul Searchers, in which Lombar sang and played lead guitar and organ. They competed in a battle of the bands at the Jacksonville Beach Auditorium but did not win. They performed as far afield as Savannah, Georgia, and Tallahassee, where they filled in for the Bitter Ind. In 1965, the Soul Searchers did some recording at Dave Plummer's Cypress Recording in Palm Valley, but no vinyl was released.

Martinich told an interviewer that the R&B group the Lemon Twisters, with Neil Seltzer on guitar, who played at their school prom in 1965, were their favorites.[168]

Lombar later joined a group called the Rowe Brothers and, in 1969, formed a Christian-rock group called King James Version (KJV), which included bassist Leon Wilkeson. The other members were keyboardist Buzzy De Loach and drummer Scotty Van Winkle. In 1969, KJV played in front of a huge audience at the Miami Rock Festival, along with the Band, Santana, B.B. King, Canned Heat, Johnny Winter and many others. KJV was short-lived, however, and Lombar, along with bassist Larry Steele, formed another short-lived group called Cornbread Davis. He and Van Winkle formed Magi with bassist Leon Wilkeson.

After the ABB made it big, many Jacksonville musicians followed in the group's footsteps, moving to Macon. Lombar was one of them, and it proved to be a wise move. He had heard that ABB roadie Joe Dan Petty from Bradenton was interested in putting together a group of his own. Petty's connections with the ABB would likely garner him a deal with Capricorn Records for his group Grinderswitch (named after a fictional town in a Minnie Pearl comedy sketch). In December 1972, Lombar headed up to Macon, hooked up with Petty and became Grinderswitch's lead singer and lead guitarist.[169]

With the help of staff producer Paul Hornsby, Grinderswitch did indeed sign with Capricorn, which released the group's debut album in 1974. Lombar stayed with Grinderswitch for nine years, recording two more albums for Capricorn, neither of which sold significant numbers, and then went on to record with various small labels until the band disbanded in 1981.[170] Grinderswitch did a lot of roadwork, opening for the likes of the ABB, Marshall Tucker Band, Wet Willie, the Charlie Daniels Band and Lynyrd Skynyrd. The group also served as singer Bonnie Bramlett's backing band during tours of Europe and Canada.

Grinderswitch, circa 1973. Dru Lombar is the fourth from the left. *Capricorn Records publicity photograph.*

Between tours with Grinderswitch, Lombar performed as a session guitarist on two albums with Capricorn singer-keyboardist Bobby Whitlock (who had worked with Eric Clapton in Derek and the Dominos and Bonnie Bramlett in Delaney and Bonnie).

Lombar returned to Jacksonville Beach, where he tried his hand as a freelance recording engineer and producer at Cypress Recording. He also went to Orlando to perform as a guest on two songs on Molly Hatchet's 1983 album, *No Guts, No Glory*, with Epic.

In the mid-1980s, a blues revival spearheaded by Robert Cray and Stevie Ray Vaughn was sweeping the nation. The time was ripe for Lombar to get back to his roots in the blues and R&B. In 1986, he formed Doctor Hector and the Groove Injectors, who became regulars on the southeastern club circuit. With Lombar fronting and playing guitar, the group soon landed a deal with Bob Greenlee's Sanford, Florida label, King Snake Records, where it released five albums.[171]

Lombar was an extremely accomplished blues player and a master of the slide guitar. He considered Duane Allman the king of that instrument.[172]

He was also a fan of Elmore James, whose "Dust My Broom" Lombar performed frequently in tribute.

In 1991, Lombar briefly reunited with former Grinderswitch cohort Larry Howard to work on Howard's gospel album, *Redeemed*, which was distributed via premier gospel label Word.

In 1992, the Groove Injectors toured Japan as the backing band for former Capricorn singer Alex Taylor (James Taylor's brother) and appeared in Paris at the Hotel Meridien. The Groove Injectors ground it out on the road for many more years until Lombar decided it was no longer financially viable.[173] Besides, his health was declining.

Lynyrd Skynyrd's reunion in the 1990s spurred a renewed interest in southern rock, and by the early 2000s, Lombar had decided to capitalize on his southern-rock credentials by reforming Grinderswitch, with himself as the leader and frontman.[174] This edition of the band included Jacksonville Beach guitarist Jack Corcoran, who now leads local group Smokestack and plays alongside young hotshot Dylan Adams (see chapter 10).

Lombar had recently established his own recording studio when he suffered a heart attack, slipped into a coma and died in September 2005. He was fifty-four years old.

Wayne Richardson, who played bass with the Groove Injectors during 1999 and 2000, said Lombar was "one of the best, a true blues man." Lombar was also a mentor: "He taught me a lot about touring and being on the road."[175]

Steve Wheeler also performed a few dates with the Groove Injectors. He said Lombar was a great singer and a great player, "very bluesy and authoritative."[176]

Lynyrd Skynyrd's story has been told so often, it is hardly necessary to reiterate it here. In 1970, local recording engineer and label owner Jim Sutton saw the group when they were called One Percent at downtown's Comic Book Club. Sutton and his business partner Tom Markham signed the group to a contract and oversaw its first recordings, one of which was the original four-minute version of "Free Bird." This version did not have the double-time ride-out with the lengthy guitar solo that made Collins famous—that would come later, after the group was discovered in an Atlanta dive, Funocchio's, by producer Al Kooper, who happened to be working in

Studio One in Doraville with members of the Atlanta Rhythm Section (who included J.R. Cobb and Robert Nix).

Skynyrd was a five-piece in 1972, when Kooper signed them to a production deal with his Sounds of the South label, distributed by MCA. Shortly after signing, bassist Leon Wilkeson decided he didn't want to be in the group—there are several stories speculating why he felt this way—and went home to Jacksonville to form a Christian-rock outfit with drummer Butch Lanham, whom he had previously played with in King James Version.[177]

In 1970, One Percent opened for Glendale, California psychedelic rockers Strawberry Alarm Clock—Jacksonville guitarist Jimmy Pitman had briefly been a member of that group (see chapter 2)—on a short southern tour. During this tour, SAC bassist Ed King mentioned to singer Ronnie Van Zant that if One Percent ever needed a guitar player or a bassist, he should give him a ring. Van Zant did exactly that when Wilkeson left. He found King working in a North Carolina bar band. King agreed to come to Jacksonville but said he had sold his car.

> I don't exactly know how Ronnie found me....I was playing this club in Greenville, and he called one day saying Leon [Wilkeson] had quit and he needed a bass player. The next day, he drove up to get me.[178]

King said Van Zant never bothered to consult the other guys in Skynyrd about hiring him and that he never felt welcomed. "Allen and Gary didn't care to have me around from the get-go—they're very competitive."[179] King told author Mark Kemp, "Ronnie Van Zant was the reason I joined that band....I didn't care anything about those other guys. I was always a better guitar player than either of them anyway."[180]

King moved into the group's rehearsal cabin near Green Cove Springs—which they called "Hell House" because it had no heating or air conditioning—where he stayed for a time, guarding the band's equipment at night. After rehearsals, he went with the group to Atlanta to play bass on its debut album, which was recorded at Studio One with producer Al Kooper.

Van Zant decided he wanted Wilkeson back on bass and sent Billy Powell and Bob Burns to the Farmbest Dairy warehouse, where Wilkeson was working, to entreat him to return.[181] "They told me they had finished the *Pronounced Leh-nerd Skin-nerd* album," Wilkeson told an interviewer, "and that Ed King really did not want to be a bass player—he wanted to play guitar—and that they did not have time to look for another bass player, so they wondered if I would oblige them and come back."[182] Wilkeson agreed. Van Zant wisely moved King to guitar, creating a "three-guitar army." King said Van Zant told him he was "the worst bass player I've ever worked with."[183] But actually King did a fine job on Skynyrd's debut.[184]

That album is mostly famous for containing a reworked, nine-minute version of "Free Bird," which features an elaborately constructed solo by Allen Collins, which was double-tracked. Collins was, of course, a Clapton acolyte. Clapton had sometimes played repetitive triplets as a sort of ostinato effect. Jacksonville drummer Scott Sisson surmised these were sort of "placeholders" Clapton used while trying to figure out what he was going to do next.[185] Duane Allman used them extensively on Wilson Pickett's Muscle Shoals recording of "Hey Jude." Jimmy Page used them, too. Influential British guitarist Alvin Lee, known for playing very quickly, made a recurrent gimmick of them, exemplified in "Going Home." Sisson joked that "Collins made a career out of them."[186]

Collins never improvised; he had his lengthy solos worked out note for note. Al Kooper told an interviewer, "Every guitar solo was played exactly the same. I have never met a band who did that."[187] Kooper had analyzed Collins's and Rossington's styles: "Allen had an Eric Clapton–like approach to his playing, while Gary's was a curious mix between Ry Cooder and Paul Kossoff of Free."[188]

Steve Wheeler said Rossington's and Collins's work in Skynyd "wasn't groundbreaking, but it fit the bill."[189]

King, on the other hand, proved to be a monster player. He said in an interview that his earliest guitar hero was James Burton, who had played in Ricky Nelson's band and later went with Elvis Presley.[190] It's probably not a coincidence that Skynyrd's sophomore album, *Second Helping*, on which King played guitar instead of bass, became the band's breakthrough. King built a signature riff over Gary Rossington's original idea that made the song "Sweet Home, Alabama" instantly memorable. Thanks in large part to King's style and virtuosity, "Sweet Home, Alabama" became a huge hit— number eight on *Billboard*'s Hot 100—and put the group on the map.

In the 1970s, Dunne noted, the credibility of any group rested on the shoulders of its lead player: "In an era when standards of musicianship were high, the lead guitarist in a rock band had to be good….The reputation of the band often rested on his instrumental prowess."[191]

Although Collins's and Rossington's work was certainly effective, neither stood out from the crowd the way King did. King had surpassed—or perhaps circumvented—slaving over the standard vocabulary most players of the day spent their lives learning. Wheeler said, "Anytime he soloed, you could immediately tell it was Ed King."[192]

Randall Hall, who worked alongside King in the second incarnation of Skynyrd from 1987 to 1994, agreed: "He had his own style," Hall said. "He could improvise. Those guys [Collins and Rossington] couldn't—their playing was all mapped out, very regimented." Hall added that King was an excellent slide player as well.[193]

One of the first things Ed King did upon arriving in Jacksonville was trade his Les Paul in for a Fender Stratocaster. He wanted his sound to stand out from the other two guitarists, who both played Gibsons.[194] "To them, it was just another guitar—no big deal—but they probably loved it because they were always louder [with their Gibsons]."[195]

King made good use of the Strat and its peculiar "squinky" tone, unique to that guitar. A lot of players call this the "quack tone." This sound was achieved by carefully manipulating the pickup selector switch, placing it between two of its three pickups. "[U]sing the switch to mix the sound of two Strat pickups produced 'snarling nasal tones that literally redefined electric guitar sound.'"[196] Jimmy Amerson said he was one of the first players in Jacksonville to do it: "I used to push a piece of a matchbook cover into the switch to hold it in place. You had to position it just right."[197]

Scott Sisson said that squinky tone—along with King's playing itself, of course—was crucial to the success of "Sweet Home, Alabama," because King's guitar was the first thing the listener heard. "It jumped right out of the speaker."[198] King's amplifier, a Fender Twin Reverb, was also an integral part of the song's tone.[199] Nonetheless, it is a truism that a guitarist's tone primarily comes not from the guitar or the amp but from way he or she picks.[200]

Former Studio One engineer Rodney Mills, who was working the "Sweet Home, Alabama" session, recalled the solo that put Skynyrd on the map. It was King's first pass, and the members of the group—and producer Al Kooper—were astounded: "The band members were in the control room when he did that, and at the end, they pretty much fell on the floor; they were just knocked out."[201]

Kooper, however, was perplexed. "You're in the wrong key, Ed!" Kooper admonished. Kooper explained in his autobiography that the song was actually in D Mixo (major mode with a flatted seventh)—common in both the blues and country—but King mistakenly assumed it was in G Ionian (the actual notes are enharmonically identical but seated in a different context). However, Kooper had to admit it was impressive: "I listened again to the solo, which was in another mode, not unlike John Coltrane's work. 'It's very progressive, Ed—I can live with it.'"[202]

Back in Florida, King moved out of Hell House and into a duplex on Rayford Street in Old Murray Hill that he shared with Van Zant and his wife, Judy.[203] As the group attained success, they were able to purchase a run-down sandwich shop on Riverside Avenue and convert it into a rehearsal space and demo studio.[204] King rented a house near Boone Park in a very pleasant old neighborhood called Avondale, three miles from the Riverside Avenue studio.[205]

Randall Hall said King was a private person and kept to himself most of the time.[206] Not being from Jacksonville, King couldn't fathom the redneck Westsider mentality.[207] King was dumbfounded by Van Zant's alcohol-fueled, Jekyll and Hyde–like episodes, which included abusive behavior toward King or anyone else who angered Van Zant. "It just got a little too nutty for me," King told interviewer Beverly Keel. "So, in the middle of the night [during a tour], I just walked out....I had gotten fed up with all the violence. I had good reason to leave."[208]

Without King, the group fell into a slump. Collins got a Stratocaster and tried to replicate King's guitar parts. Still, the group realized they needed a third guitarist to fill out the sound they were famous for. At one point, Jeff Carlisi, who attended some rehearsals at Hell House, may have been considered.

Skynyrd had hired a female trio to sing backing vocals, one of whom was Cassie Gaines from Miami, Oklahoma. Her brother, Steve, she said, was a phenomenal player. Born in Miami, Oklahoma, in 1949—on the very same day Ed King was born in California—Gaines's earliest musical inspiration was the Beatles. He had worked with several bands before joining Skynyrd, most notably Crawdad, which had relocated to Macon, where they recorded an album at Capricorn Studios, featuring Gaines on vocals in 1975. When he left that group to join Skynyrd, another Oklahoma musician, Ace Moreland, took his place as frontman in Crawdad.[209]

Gaines breathed new life into Skynyrd, bringing in not only fresh blood but also new song ideas, amazing guitar techniques and a stellar singing voice. He was a "triple threat." Van Zant said the other members would "all be in his shadow one day."[210] Not only an amazing talent, Gaines was, from all available reports, an exceptionally nice guy as well.[211] He was brought into the group in 1976 in time to perform on a live album, *One More from the Road*, and a new studio album, *Street Survivors*, issued in August 1977.

LEON WILKESON   ARTIMUS PYLE   ALLEN COLLINS   GARY ROSSINGTON   STEVE GAINES
                                   BILLY POWELL
                                   RONNIE VAN ZANT

L Y N Y R D ■ S K Y N Y R D   .MCA RECORDS

Lynyrd Skynyrd, circa 1976. Steve Gaines (*right*). *MCA Records publicity photograph.*

Jacksonville guitarist Page Matherson said of all the Skynyrd guitarists' work, he liked Gaines's the most. "Steve Gaines blew me away," he said, "He was better than [Rossington and Collins] put together."[212]

John Moss, who worked with Gaines in Crawdad, said, "I have never seen anybody get so good on the guitar."[213]

Skynyrd drummer Artimus Pyle said Gaines never took his guitar off. "He slept with that thing." Pyle went so far as to say Gaines was "the best thing that ever happened to Skynyrd."[214]

Gaines and his wife, Teresa, moved to Fleming Island, not far from Van Zant's new home on Brickyard Road in Doctor's Inlet. But his time in the Jacksonville area—and with Skynyrd—was brief, fewer than eighteen months. He was one of the three band members—along with his sister, Cassie, and Ronnie Van Zant—killed in Skynyrd's plane crash on October 20, 1977.

6

SOUTHERN ROCK REDUX

W e've seen how the Ventures in 1960 and the Beatles in 1964 inspired thousands of budding electric guitarists all over the world. By 1968, a new wave of players had sprung up in Jacksonville, many of them Eric Clapton clones. Clapton was, in a way, the godfather of southern rock.[215] "Don Barnes, who started out in 38 Special as a guitarist said, "We all [Westside guitarists] wanted to be Clapton.""[216]

Many, including Dickey Betts, would borrow pages from Clapton's book. Allen Collins certainly was not averse to recycling some of Clapton's ideas, said guitarist Mike Owings, who worked with Collins in a reformed version of the Allen Collins Band. Owings described a 1984 rehearsal that took place at Collins's home: "In the middle of my solo, Allen grabs my guitar by the neck and yells, 'Quit stealing my licks!' I told him, 'I'll stop stealing your licks when you stop stealing Eric Clapton's.' He laughed and said, 'You got me, man.'"

Page Matherson was another fan of Clapton's; in fact, he had to learn Clapton's solos for the Daybreakers, who played Cream favorites. "I had 'Crossroads' down pretty good," he said.[217]

Jimi Hendrix—who, like Clapton, emerged from the London blues rock scene—also lit a fire under many local players. Jacksonville guitarists Randall Hall and Steve Wheeler both saw Hendrix perform at the Jacksonville Memorial Coliseum in 1967, when the Jimi Hendrix Experience opened for the Monkees. Both said witnessing Hendrix was a life-changing experience. Wheeler said Hendrix did not rely heavily on theatrics at this show; "he just played his ass off."[218]

Texas guitarist Johnny Winter was a big inspiration for many. Winter was one of Paul Glass's idols, along with Hendrix, Clapton, Mike Bloomfield and Duane Allman, more or less in that order—all heavily steeped in the blues. Like Glass and Randall Hall, Matherson was struck by Bloomfield's playing: "I wore out the *Super Session* album."[219] Duane Allman was still an obscure figure in 1968, but local boys in the know were aware of his work.

If, by chance, local players wanted to find out where Clapton, Hendrix, Page and the others got their ideas from, they might have dug up some tracks by B.B. King, Albert King or Luther Tucker. But generally it was the English blues-rockers who lit their fires. Many of the British players were steeped in southern styles, even country—the Rolling Stones, who started off as a blues band, had, by 1968, imbibed a good deal of country influences. Ironically, many if not most of Jacksonville's southern rockers were bringing British blues-rock back home to the South.

Southern rock—a nebulous term at best—was a blend of styles that included the blues, country, gospel and even some jazz, all combined within a rock perspective. Not all southern-rock bands sounded alike, but most had these components in varying proportions. Even a cursory look at southern rock will demonstrate that it was almost entirely based on the electric guitar. As with British blues rockers, southern-rock singers often took a backseat to the guitar gods.

FIVE YEARS AFTER TRYING to pass himself off as the former rhythm guitarist of the Doors (see chapter 3), Dave Hlubek was looking to form a new band. A navy brat who had moved to Jacksonville from California in the mid-1960s (he was born in Jacksonville, however), Hlubek attended Forrest High School alongside Allen Collins and Leon Wilkeson. His first group, Mynd Garden, included future Molly Hatchet bassist Tim Lindsey.

In 1971, Hlubek was trying out guitars at Paulus Music when he ran into former Virginia Beach resident Steve Holland. Hlubek and Holland decided to join forces to form a new, guitar-driven group—as if Jacksonville didn't already have enough of them. In 2001, Hlubek told interviewer Michael Buffalo Smith:

> *I heard this voice behind me saying, "That guitar really sucks." I turned around and asked who he was, and he said, "I'm Steve Holland. Wanna*

start a band?"...We started rehearsing that very afternoon, and that band went on to become Molly Hatchet.[220]

This new group, Bandit, with a continually shifting cast of performers, played the local bars and nightclubs before settling on the name Molly Hatchet, an apocryphal prostitute who ostensibly enjoyed a propensity for beheading her johns.

A third guitarist, Duane Roland from Indiana, was added, but he left shortly afterward, replaced by Kenny Niblick. Not long afterward, the group added singer Danny Joe Brown, who had sung for Bobby Ingram's group Rum Creek. The group's original drummer, Freddy Bianco, left in 1975, replaced by Memphis native Bruce Crump.

Singer Donnie Van Zant of 38 Special recommended Hatchet to manager Pat Armstrong. Armstrong, by this time, was in Macon, where he was attending law school. He went to see Hatchet perform at a gig in Knoxville in 1976 and signed the group to management, production and publishing deals.

Armstrong brought Ronnie Van Zant and Skynyrd soundman Kevin Elson to see his new charges perform in Daytona Beach. Impressed, Van Zant offered to produce some demos for them and use his connections to shop them to record labels.[221] Van Zant and Elson brought Hatchet into Skynyrd's studio on Riverside Avenue, where they helped the group tighten up their arrangements. "Ronnie made the songs on our first album make sense," Hlubek told an interviewer.[222] Van Zant was ready to go bat for Molly Hatchet at MCA Records.[223] Unfortunately, he would not live to do so.

Armstrong had Hatchet cut some demos in Jacksonville at Tom Markam's Warehouse studio (Markham had coproduced Skynyrd's earliest recordings alongside Jim Sutton at Norm Vincent Studio). Hatchet later went to Atlanta to record some tracks at the Sound Pit. It just so happened that Epic Records' staff producer Tom Werman liked working at that studio. Armstrong arranged for the group to set up in the studio and do a live audition for Werman. Werman was impressed, and Epic signed the band. Hatchet recorded its 1978 debut album at the Sound Pit, which Werman mixed at the Record Plant in Los Angeles.[224] Derek Kinner wrote:

That eponymous record...was obviously spawned from the same primordial soup as Lynyrd Skynyrd and 38 Special. But at the same time, it was harder, rougher, grittier, unapologetically blue-collar, [as] if Skynyrd were taken over by hardcore bikers.[225]

Molly Hatchet, 1978. *Epic Records publicity photograph.*

Skynyrd had been devastated by its plane crash a year earlier, and the Allman Brothers Band was in total disarray. Who would become the kingpins of southern rock? Although there were other contenders, such as the Marshall Tucker Band, the Atlanta Rhythm Section and the Outlaws, being from the same neighborhood where the ABB and Sknyryd emerged gave these Westside boys a slight edge on the competition.[226]

The Hatchet members had taken more than musical cues from Lynyrd Skynyrd; they also borrowed Skynyrd's image-building technique, which meant garnering publicity as hard-drinking, brawling renegades, which almost became a trademark—and a trap—for southern rockers in general.[227]

Hatchet's three-guitar approach, plus strong showmanship from singer Danny Joe Brown, proved effective, and the group earned a gold album (sales of five hundred thousand units). Its follow-up album, *Flirtin' with Disaster*, did even better, selling around two million copies. Hatchet was huge.

Hlubek, the group's leader, appeared to be its guitar god, but Steve Wheeler said Duane Roland was actually the best guitarist in the group. "His work was the most articulate and precise." Much like Rossington and Collins from Skynyrd, Wheeler said, the Hatchet guitarists "were really well-rehearsed and worked well together." Their playing was effective, but none of it reached the virtuosity of Ed King or Steve Gaines.[228]

Despite—or perhaps because of—Molly Hatchet's success, the group began coming unglued. These guys really were flirting with disaster. Massive

China Sky, 1988. *Left to right*: Bobby Ingram, Ron Perry and Richard Smith. *PARC Records publicity photograph, by Wiley and Flynn; courtesy of Ron Perry.*

amounts of cocaine and alcohol began warping their perspectives. One by one, the original members started dropping out. Brown was the first to leave, forming his own band in 1980 with Jacksonville guitarists Bobby Ingram, his former bandmate in Rum Creek, and Wheeler.

After the Danny Joe Brown Band (DJBB) abruptly imploded, Brown returned to Molly Hatchet, gradually bringing in Ingram along with Detroit keyboardist John Galvin, both of whom had been in the DJBB. Members came and went. Some came back, left and then came back again. Things got so outlandish the band began to resemble the comedic fictional group Spinal Tap.[229] Holland and, later, Hlubek, the group's founders, eventually walked away. For several years, Duane Roland remained the sole original member. He retired in 1995, licensing and later selling the rights to the band's name to Ingram, who carried on the group's mission.

Ingram, at different points, added guitarists Erik Lundgren, a phenomenal player formerly of the Johnny Van Zant Band who had studied with Robert Conti, and Brian Bassett, formerly of the Pittsburgh funk-rock group Wild Cherry (Bassett played the solo on that group's 1976 hit "Play That Funky Music").

As of this writing, Molly Hatchet has no original members left, and the group which built its reputation as a three-guitar army has only one guitarist. How then is it possible for Hatchet to recreate its classic sound? "Galvin plays guitar parts on a synthesizer," said Jacksonville guitarist-vocalist Ron Perry. Perry was in China Sky with Ingram back in 1988 and is himself a formidable player, singer and songwriter. "But it's not the same."[230]

Things did not go well for founders Dave Hlubek and Steve Holland after they left Hatchet. Back in Jacksonville, Hlubek and former Rossington-Collins Band singer/guitarist Barry Lee Harwood, who wrote and sang that group's 1980 hit, "Don't Misunderstand Me," formed the Hlubek-Harwood Band. Very little happened with this project, drummer Scott Sisson said, primarily because Hlubek failed to show up to rehearsals.[231] Hlubek told an interviewer, "I had a horrendous cocaine problem."[232] By about 1988, Hlubek was working a day job, painting racing stripes on Corvettes.[233] In 1989, he hooked up with former Blackfoot drummer Jakson Spires to form the Dixie Allstars (later the Southern-Rock Allstars). Hlubek stayed with that group until 2003, when he was replaced by former Hatchet bandmate Duane Roland.

Things were arguably worse for Holland, who found himself staying with friends until he landed in a nursing home with a cognitive impairment. He died in 2020.

Hlubek died in 2017, as did bassist Banner Thomas. Roland died in 2006. Drummer Bruce Crump died in 2015, and singer Danny Joe Brown died in 2005. Every original member is gone, as are several replacements: singers Jimmy Farrar and Phil McCormick died in 2018 and 2019, respectively, along with bassists Buzzy Meekins and Riff West, both in 2013. An overly superstitious person might conclude that the band members were under some sort of curse—as if the ghost of Hatchet Molly had come back to wreak her revenge.

Still, Bobby Ingram is determined to carry on the band's tradition. The group stays busy, mostly performing at outdoor shows and festivals. They remain fairly popular in Europe and record for the German label SPV.

7

MEANWHILE, DOWN IN GAINESVILLE

As a teenager, Mike Campbell was very attached to his guitar. Sometimes he wouldn't even go to the bathroom without it. His neighborhood pal Mike Bell used to go to the Campbells' house after school in Jacksonville's Northside, where they would give each other pointers. Bell recalled:

> One afternoon, I went to his house to jam. His mother let me in and said he'd be right out. As I sat in his bedroom playing my guitar, he came out of the bathroom with his guitar in hand. I looked at him, puzzled. He shrugged and said, "What else would I do sitting there?"[234]

Born in Panama City, Florida, Michael Wayne Campbell grew up in Northside's Riverview District, where he attended Jean Ribault High School, along with Bell. Campbell's first guitar was a Harmony archtop acoustic his mother bought at a pawn shop for fifteen dollars.[235] He told an interviewer the first song he learned to play was Bob Dylan's version of "Baby, Let Me Follow You Down."[236] He could not possibly have imagined that, one day, he would actually find himself working with his idol.

Starting out as a folkie, Campbell changed direction after seeing the Beatles on the *Ed Sullivan Show* in early 1964. The Fab Four fired his obsession with the electric guitar, as it did for thousands of adolescent boys, particularly those in Jacksonville.[237]

Campbell's air force father and his mother divorced when he was fifteen; his mom had a tough time making ends meet. In 1964, Campbell could not manage to scrape together five dollars for a ticket to see the Beatles at the Gator Bowl, much less a few hundred for a decent electric.[238] However, during a tour of Okinawa, his father sent home a sixty-dollar Japanese Guyatone, and young Campbell set about learning Beatles songs, along with those of the Byrds, the Rolling Stones, Chuck Berry and, of course, the obligatory "Walk Don't Run" by the Ventures.[239]

Mike Bell was having a tough time figuring out how to play the blues, so he lent Campbell two albums, one by the Grateful Dead and another by the Paul Butterfield Blues Band, which featured Mike Bloomfield on lead guitar. Bell said Campbell had it all figured by the next day. "He showed me the 'blues box' [pentatonic scale] he'd worked out and insisted it was really simple—and of course it was." Neither guitarist owned an amplifier at this point.[240]

Campbell was a shy kid, Bell said. He was not keen on networking with other musicians. Bell dragged Campbell to meet some friends who had formed a jug-band collective in the Riverside District.[241] Campbell said he was bolstered by the fact that these musicians thought he could play.[242]

He did not, however, make himself part of Jacksonville's booming electric guitar scene and apparently never played in a local band. Almost no one connected with the 1960s teen music milieu recalls meeting Campbell or even hearing about him during his time in Jacksonville. It probably didn't help that he was sheepish about his low-budget guitar. Owning a crappy guitar was the veritable kiss of death for young players; there was an unwritten yet ironclad rule that said without a professional instrument, you would be branded as an amateur or worse.[243]

Campbell had planned to attend university—he had garnered good enough grades—but in order to stay by his mom and his siblings, he felt he should attend a two-year program at Florida Junior College in Jacksonville and perhaps transfer to a university later. However, a high school counselor advised him to head straight to the University of Florida (UF) in Gainesville, seventy-three miles southwest of home, where he signed up for general-education courses in order to stall for time while deciding what his major might be.[244]

Gainesville opened doors for Campbell in ways he never could have imagined. First of all, the competition between the guitar players there was not as cutthroat as it had been in Jacksonville.

While living in the student dorms at UF, Campbell met bass player Hal Maull and drummer Randall Marsh; the three formed a group called Dead or Alive. However, the blues-based power trio—a common format at the time—didn't garner many bookings. "We played around the college for free," Campbell told an interviewer, "and did some women's clubs here and there." When Maull moved to Hawaii, the group fizzled.[245]

Campbell and Marsh were sharing a secluded house on the outskirts of town when Campbell spotted an advertisement for a drummer posted on a musicians' board at Lipham's Music.[246] "I thought it would be great to get him [Marsh] out of the house," Campbell told biographer Warren Zanes. "I was kind of sick of him."[247] Three longhaired guys from a local roots rock band called Mudcrutch came over to hear Marsh play.

Mudcrutch was an outgrowth of the teen group the Epics, spearheaded by an extremely driven local man named Tom Petty along with guitarist Tom Leadon, the younger brother of country-rock pioneer Bernie Leadon, a founding member of the Flying Burrito Brothers and the Eagles. Petty had taken guitar lessons at Lipham's from virtuoso Don Felder, who later became a member of the Eagles. However, Petty played bass with the Epics and Mudcrutch and was not yet the group's lead singer.

Bassist Petty, singer Jim Lenahan and guitarist Tom Leadon showed up to hear Marsh play.[248] The group was also looking for a second guitarist. Marsh mentioned that his housemate was a good player and went to the back room, where Campbell was reading, to invite him to sit in.

There are multiple, perhaps excessively colorful, accounts of this momentous meeting—at least two from Campbell himself and one from Petty—but Tom Leadon's seems the most plausible:

> He [Campbell] *did not look like a professional musician, because he had short hair and a cheap Japanese guitar. In those days, the Japanese guitars had very bad reputations as being not much more than toys....When he came into the room, Tom and I gave each other a look that was like, "Oh, gosh, here we go"—in other words, we thought it might be pretty bad.*

Leadon soon noted, however, that Campbell knew what he was doing:

> *So, before we really even talked to Mike, I started showing him the chord changes to some of our original arrangements, mostly country-rock [songs], which were written by Tom. I noticed right away that he was learning them quickly and that he was able to play steady rhythm....After we had taught them several songs, Randall Marsh asked Mike if he would play "Johnny B. Goode."...[H]e really played it great. By the end of the song, we were all really excited, so we asked them both to be in the group.[249]*

Tom Petty meets Mike Campbell in Gainesville, 1970. Campbell can be seen on the right holding a Guyatone guitar. *Photograph by Red Slater; used with permission.*

Mudcrutch snagged a six-night-a-week booking at Dub's Steer Room, working alongside topless dancers. After a few days of working until 1:45 a.m. and getting up early for classes, Campbell dropped out of UF. He also decided it was time to ditch the Guyatone. He went to Lipham Music and traded it in for a used Fender Stratocaster. However, he didn't like the Strat, so while the group was performing in Birmingham, Alabama, he bought a Gibson Firebird, a favorite of Eric Clapton's (and Allen Collins's). [250]

Campbell and Leadon bonded as guitarists, working out the dual-lead strategies that were integral to the group's country-rock style:

> *I recognized right away that Mike was an excellent lead guitarist, and I remember just about the first thing I ever said to him after* [he and Marsh] *joined the group: I walked right over to him and proposed that we split the solos and fills fifty-fifty.* [251]

A good example of Campbell and Leadon's work together is Mudcrutch's first single, "Up in Mississippi," recorded in 1971 in Miami by Criteria's in-house producer-engineer Ron Albert, whose list of credits already included Jacksonville's 31st of February and Eric Clapton's group Derek and the Dominos, both of whom had included guest guitarist Duane Allman.

The intertwining electric guitars were essential to Mudcrutch's style, which sounds like a hybrid of the Flying Burrito Brothers' and the Allman Brothers Band's styles; in other words, they were a combination of East Coast and West Coast roots-rock. Tom Leadon insisted, however, that the ABB was not a significant influence on himself or Campbell. Much like the Jacksonville group Cowboy, Mudcrutch was more of a California-style country-rock group. [252] "Our influences were more from the Byrds, the Flying Burrito Brothers,

Dillard and Clark, Poco and other Los Angeles groups."[253] In addition, Tom's older brother, Bernie Leadon, a leading figure in the West Coast country-rock movement, was giving the members of Mudcrutch advice.

Mudcrutch's members were fans of Jacksonville's Lynyrd Skynyrd. The two groups helped each other get gigs; when Skynyrd came to Gainesville, they served as Mudcrutch's opening act and vice versa when Mudcrutch performed in Jacksonville.[254] Mudcrutch even followed the ABB and Skynyrd to Macon, where they hooked up with the Armstrong Agency for regional booking; however, Macon—the headquarters of so-called southern rock—turned out not to be a good fit for the group.

In 1972, Tom Leadon, becoming impatient with the group's progress, was invited to join his brother Bernie in Los Angeles. So he split.[255]

Leadon was replaced by Danny Roberts from Lakeland. Roberts had been performing around the region with a prominent trio called Power, for which Mudcrutch had opened some shows. Roberts also sang and wrote songs.

Musician-writer Jeff Calder, who had known Roberts since their teen band days in Lakeland, asserted that Mudcrutch was not even in the same league as Power:

> By no means had Mudcrutch been a bad band, but they were nebulous.... That changed when Danny Roberts moved to Gainesville. His professional experience was of greater compass. He helped the band organize more serious demo sessions, and the group's songwriting improved almost overnight. He alternated bass and guitar with Tom, and, with the additional support of Danny's British blues-influenced vocals, the music of Mudcrutch finally received its first dimension. By April 1973, their new authority was undeniable.[256]

Roberts was also instrumental in helping Mudcrutch score a deal in Los Angeles. He drove Petty and the group's roadie/sound man, Keith "Duke" McAllister, on a cross-country reconnaissance mission in his Volkswagen van. Tom Leadon was already in Los Angeles, working with Linda Ronstadt, and the Mudcrutch boys had a good music business connection by way of Tom's brother Bernie, who was flying high with the Eagles.[257]

But they didn't need help. Armed with a reel of demos, Petty, Roberts and McAllister dutifully pounded the pavement and, within forty-eight hours, garnered positive responses from multiple prospects, eventually settling with Hollywood-based Shelter Records, headed by singer-writer-arranger-pianist Leon Russell and producer Denny Cordell.

Roberts considered Mudcrutch a democracy and expected his songs and voice to be featured alongside Petty's. After all, plenty of groups had multiple lead singers and writers; this is the way Mudcrutch had operated since Roberts had come aboard. However, producer Cordell—perhaps unknown to the other band members—wanted Petty front and center exclusively.[258]

Roberts, becoming impatient and disgruntled, departed and was replaced by Tampa bassist Charlie Souza, formerly of the Tropics. Souza, too, insisted on contributing unwelcome material to the proceedings: "It was one I wrote about a spaceman and a UFO coming down," Souza told Warren Zanes. "Tom thought I was nuts.…So, there was a little edginess."[259] Petty and Cordell decided Souza was not a good fit, so he returned to Florida.

Roberts returned to Florida for a while and then went back to Los Angeles, where he worked with Shelter artists Dwight Twilley and Phil Seymour, eventually returning to Florida, where he joined up with Jacksonville slide guitar prodigy Derek Trucks. Roberts fronted and played guitar with the Derek Trucks Band in the early 1990s, alongside Jacksonville drummer Derek Hess. Roberts lived in St. Augustine, forty miles southeast of Jacksonville, for seventeen years.

By the mid-1970s, things had gotten chaotic for Mudcrutch. The group seemed to be chasing their tails; the members were dispirited, and they finally fizzled. Cordell, who was hemorrhaging money, decided to drop the group. However, he offered to keep Petty under contract as a solo artist. Petty was—wisely—adamant about keeping Campbell at his side and negotiated support payments for both. Campbell, in turn, stood by Petty through thick and thin. His commitment would pay off one thousand times over.

Meanwhile, Mudcrutch keyboardist Benmont Tench assembled a new project with guitarist Jeff Jourard, bassist Ron Blair and drummer Stan Lynch, all of whom were from Gainesville. After cutting some tracks with session players, Petty decided he didn't want to be a solo artist after all. He attended a rehearsal of Tench's group and decided to adopt the outfit as his own, bringing Campbell in with him. Petty, however, decided three guitarists were one too many, so Jourard was let go (he stayed in Los Angeles, eventually helping form the Motels).

The new group, christened Tom Petty and the Heartbreakers—the name was Cordell's idea—went to work recording for Shelter, but its progress was excruciatingly slow. The group finally broke through in a big way after obtaining a high-powered manager, former Elliot Roberts associate Tony Dimitriades, in 1978 and parting with Shelter a year later. *Damn the Torpedoes*, produced by Jimmy Iovine and released in 1979 via MCA—the same label that handled Lynyrd Skynyrd—became an instant classic and a multiplatinum seller that launched Petty and his group into the upper echelons of stardom.

Campell had been writing with Petty since joining Mudcrutch, building a studio in his San Fernando Valley home, where he started cutting backing tracks. He would submit these to Petty, who would, in turn, write lyrics and melodies ("toplines"). Campbell cowrote several Heartbreakers hits, such as "Refugee," "Here Comes My Girl," "Don't Come Around Here No More," "You Got Lucky" and many others. All totaled, Campbell wrote or cowrote thirty-six songs for the Heartbreakers and/or Tom Petty, including a Petty duet with Stevie Nicks, "Stop Draggin' My Heart Around."

Campbell originally wrote "Boys of Summer" for the Heartbreakers in 1984, but Petty didn't dig it. Campbell heard that former Eagles singer Don Henley was looking for material, so he brought him the backing tracks. Henley modified the chords on the chorus—putting it into a major key for relief—and took the song to number five on *Billboard*'s Hot 100.

The following list of other artists whom Campbell wrote or cowrote for is impressive.

- Stevie Nicks
- Fleetwood Mac
- Robin Zander
- Lone Justice
- George Jones
- Dixie Chicks
- Wallflowers

In 2007, Tom Petty decided to put together a Mudcrutch reunion with a four-piece edition of the group; the band included Petty, Mike Campbell, Tom Leadon and Randall Marsh. Former singer Jim Lenahan, who had been with the group from 1970 to 1971, refused to discuss the reunion and his omission from it.[260] Later members Danny Roberts (1972–75) and Charlie Souza (1975) were not consulted. Roberts was shocked to discover that his image had been airbrushed out of one of Mudcrutch's 1974 publicity photographs. "I try not to be bitter, but I can't but be a little hurt by such an intentional snub," Roberts said in an interview. "I thought Tom was bigger than that."[261]

Another Mudcrutch reunion followed in 2016, which comprised the final studio recordings Petty made before his death in 2017.

Petty's demise has not deterred Campbell's career. He has continued to serve as an in-demand session player and songwriter. Campbell has been successful beyond his wildest dreams, having worked with some of his childhood idols, like Dylan, Roger McGuinn and George Harrison. He also worked with the supergroup the Traveling Wilburys alongside Petty, Dylan, Harrison, Roy Orbison and Jeff Lynne. Campbell's contributions as a session player are astounding.

- Stevie Nicks (Campbell appears on eight albums.)
- Bob Dylan (Campbell appears on four albums.)
- Don Henley (Campbell appears on three albums.)
- Warren Zevon (Campbell appears on three albums.)
- Neil Diamond (Campbell appears on three albums.)
- Jackson Browne (Campbell appears on two albums.)
- Linda Ronstadt
- Chris Stapleton
- Roy Orbison
- Joe Cocker
- Philip Bailey
- Randy Crawford
- Melba Moore
- Matthew Sweet
- Susanna Hoffs
- Stephanie Mills
- Rob Thomas
- Paul Carrack
- Mary J. Blige
- Michael McDonald
- Tracy Chapman
- Taj Mahal
- Randy Newman
- Aretha Franklin
- Bob Seger
- John Prine
- Dixie Chicks

One of the reasons Campbell remains in high demand is his superb taste as a player. Steve Wheeler said, "He never overplays, and his stuff is memorable and inventive." Guitarist Gary Powell agrees: "He's one of those guys who always plays for the benefit of the song—seems like he just knows what needs to be there."

In 2018, Campbell was invited to join Fleetwood Mac. In his seventies, he continues to remain busy, touring with and fronting his own group, the Dirty Knobs.

8

SOUTHERN-ROCK REFUGEES

After ten years of being the predominant style around Jacksonville, southern rock had become a caricature. Musicians in Jacksonville who were sick of playing "Free Bird" struggled to get away from it—as did some of the southern rockers themselves, although not always voluntarily.

But back in 1974, 38 Special enjoyed an edge on the competition: the group's lead singer, Donnie Van Zant, was Skynyrd singer Ronnie Van Zant's younger brother, and the group benefited not only from his advice but also from his connections.

Donnie, who attended Lake Shore Junior High, had been in the music business longer than Ronnie had. Although he was more than three years younger than Ronnie, he formed his first group, Sons of Satan, in 1965, a year before Ronnie started with Rick Doeschler's group Us. Sons of Satan— later to become Sons of Satin in response to objections from Van Zant's mother, Marion Van Zant—included Westside guitarists Del Sumner and Ronnie Lee. Drummer Steve Brookins, also from the neighborhood and who later performed with 38 Special, recalled to Larry Steele:

> I was riding my bicycle by Del's house, where we had the [band's equipment] trailer parked. I saw the back door of the trailer was half open as I rode by....I went to my dad and Mr. Sumner and said, "Hey! I think somebody's in our trailer!" We went out there, where my dad, with his flashlight, shines it into the trailer and says, "Hey! Who's in there?" Then I hear this kid's voice, say, "I'm just looking for my guitar." The kid was Don Barnes.[262]

Steele cited this episode as an example of how important it was for a young player to own a good-quality instrument: "To be taken seriously, you had to at least show up with a quality instrument. The extremes some would go to just to be able to play were without limitation."[263]

Barnes lived across the Cedar River from the Van Zants' neighborhood.[264] He later became one of the two guitarists in 38 Special and, eventually, its lead singer. Donnie Van Zant, who mimicked his brother—and Gregg Allman—was the frontman of 38 Special and the group's main draw. Still, a band was considered only as good as its lead guitarist(s).[265]

By 1976, Skynyrd had scored several hits, and Ronnie used his network to hook 38 Special up with a well-connected manager. First, he took them to former Skynyrd comanager Pat Armstrong in Macon, who passed on the group, saying he didn't think their material was strong enough—and he would be proven right.[266] Ronnie then took the group to Skynyrd's manager, Peter Rudge, at Sir Productions. Rudge, who had also worked with the Who and the Rolling Stones, deployed his formidable clout to land 38 Special a deal with Los Angeles–based A&M Records.

However, by 1977, when 38 Special released its first album—produced in Connecticut by hit songwriter-guitarist-keyboardist Dan Hartman— southern rock was already on the way out.

Doggedly determined, the group stayed the course for one more album. Steve Penhollow wrote, "Unfortunately, strict adherence to the southern-rock tradition did not bring [38 Special] commercial success."[267]

Barnes said in an interview that it finally became obvious the members were wasting their energies mimicking the successful southern-rock acts of the day. "People were saying 'Skynyrd Junior' and all that," Barnes said. "Ronnie came to us and said, 'Quit trying to be a clone of what's already out there.'"[268]

There were a couple of Skynyd-esque numbers on 38 Special's eponymous debut, but much if not most of the album echoed the West Coast country-rock of the Eagles, Poco and Jackson Browne. After two unsuccessful albums, A&M executives issued an ultimatum: get some hits or get gone. "We went back to Jacksonville and were standing in the unemployment line for a while," Barnes told an interviewer. "That was embarrassing."[269]

For 38 Special's third—and what might have been final—album, the group hired a new producer, Rodney Mills, who had worked on four Skynyrd albums at Studio One in Doraville, outside of Atlanta, as well as several albums by the Atlanta Rhythm Section. The group's third album was already in the can when manager Mark Spector, a former A&M executive,

"38" SPECIAL

PARAGON AGENCY
1019 Walnut Street
P.O.Box 4408
Macon, Ga. 31208
(912)742-3381

The band 38 Special, circa 1975. *Left to right*: Jack Grondin (drums), Ken Lyons (bass), Don Barnes (guitar), Jeff Carlisi (guitar), Steve Brookins (drums) and Donnie Van Zant (vocals). *Paragon Agency publicity photograph.*

gave them a tape of a song written by Chicago musician Jim Peterik, a member of the Atlantic Records act Survivor. "Rockin' into the Night," had been left off Survivor's debut album.

Barnes explained, "You're about to lose the deal, and the record company sends you a song, you figure, 'We'll try anything at this point.'"[270] Donnie Van Zant decided he didn't want to sing "Rockin' into the Night," so Barnes, who had never sung lead with the group, stepped forward—at Carlisi's suggestion—to handle the vocal chores.[271] Van Zant later took a shot at it, but the group decided Barnes's version was superior.[272] His voice was powerful and exhibited suitable range. From this point on, Barnes sang on all the group's fifteen top-forty singles (except 1988's "Second Chance," which was sung by replacement singer Max Carl).

The single "Rockin' into the Night," released in October 1979, achieved a respectable spot at fifty-seven on *Billboard*'s Hot 100 singles chart, and the sales of the album were encouraging enough to convince A&M to re-sign the group. More new material in the same vein was needed, so Spector suggested Barnes and Carlisi should get together with Peterik in Chicago to do some writing.[273] Carlisi contributed a staccato chord progression that sounded a lot like the new-wave group the Cars, and the three turned it into "Hold on Loosely," which sailed to number twenty-seven in early 1981.[274]

Carlisi's fluid soloing on "Hold on Loosely" would cement his reputation as a guitar god. It's a classic solo, said Steve Wheeler, who had to learn it note for note in order to play it in local bands. "The influences in it are mostly from Barry Bailey [of the Atlanta Rhythm Section]," he said. There are also elements of Dicky Betts's work, along with some from Allen Collins and Leslie West.[275]

Carlisi has acknowledged his debt to Bailey. While he was an architecture student at Georgia Tech, he encountered Bailey sitting in with Skynyrd at Funocchio's in Atlanta. Just before 38 Special was set to record its third album at Studio One, where Bailey was a first-call session player, Carlisi visited the studio. Bailey and engineer-producer Mills were working on guitar parts. "I really got a grasp on the discipline Barry had as a player and how he played for the song," Carlisi told an interviewer. "That was an important educational event for me." Carlisi even had a Les Paul Deluxe almost exactly like Bailey's, which Bailey had bought from J.R. Cobb, a fellow member of the Atlanta Rhythm Section and former Jacksonville resident (see chapter 2).[276]

The son of a U.S. Navy officer, Carlisi was born in Queens and spent the early part of his life in Boston. His family came to Jacksonville when he was nine years old, moving to Cedar Hills, only blocks from Allen Collins's house. He was interested in music, so his parents urged him to take piano lessons; instead, he started with the accordion, which he quickly abandoned. He switched to guitar using an old, no-name acoustic that his father had picked up from a family member.

After seeing the Beatles on the *Ed Sullivan Show* in early 1964, he knew he had to get an electric. "It wasn't their hair; it wasn't the screaming fans; it was the electric guitars [that got me]." He talked his parents into getting him a dual-pickup Gibson Melody Maker—the same guitar that Mods member Allen Collins owned—from Fred Paulus at Paulus Music downtown.[277] Carlisi met Collins in 1966 and would pedal his bike over to Collins's house to trade licks. When Collins later got a Firebird, Carlisi, too, went out and got one.[278]

Carlisi said he didn't have any specific guitar heroes when he started out—it was more about learning songs. Of course, he started with the usual fare: "Little Black Egg," "Gloria" and several Rolling Stones tunes. At some point, he reached back to the past to learn some Ventures material and became impressed with Nokie Edwards's work. He was surprised an honored, he said, when his guitar teacher Terry Cosgrove invited him to play rhythm guitar with his group, the Summer Sons.[279]

When pop morphed into "rock," Carlisi, like most other players in the area, spent a lot of time learning Eric Clapton licks. Some studied Hendrix's work, but as Carlisi pointed out, Hendrix's stylings were too idiosyncratic for most young players. It wasn't that his playing was terribly difficult, it was just hard to understand. Clapton's playing made more sense. Other influences for Carlisi were Duane Allman and Dickey Betts (more so Allman, he said), Leslie West of Mountain, Kal David of Illinois Speed Press and, later, Brian May of Queen and Larry Carlton.[280]

Carlisi hooked up with rock groups, such as Marshmellow Steamshovel, Doomsday Refreshment Committee and, in 1970, Sweet Rooster, which included three future members of 38 Special. In 1970, he left for Atlanta to attend the Georgia Institute of Technology, where he studied architecture. While living in Atlanta, he fell into a bluegrass and country band led by one of his professors and learned to play Dobro and pedal steel.

Meanwhile, Donnie Van Zant formed another group with Don Barnes on guitar, Steve Brookins on drums and Larry Steele on bass. Barnes wanted to bring in another guitarist. Steele had recommended Randall Hall, but the others had been talking to Carlisi, who was about to graduate. Steele did not want Carlisi in the group because he felt Carlisi had not made the ultimate sacrifice by quitting school like the others had. Steele said he felt it would be too easy for Carlisi to walk away when the going got tough. So Steele left the group, which would become 38 Special, and Ken Lyons was brought in as his replacement.[281] Proving Steele wrong, Carlisi toughed it out—through thick and thin— for twenty-three years.

True to his word, Ronnie Van Zant helped his brother's new group break into the big-time, and after some early trials and tribulations, success finally beckoned for 38 Special. However, the same year "Hold on Loosely" came out, MTV—the new-wave–leaning cable channel—exploded on the national scene, changing the face of pop music. This was a death knell for southern rock, and the members of 38 Special were astute enough to see it coming, unlike the members of Molly Hatchet and Blackfoot. Suddenly, southern rock was an anachronism. The group moved Van Zant over to rhythm guitar; he still sang his southern-rock anthems in the group's live shows and on album cuts, but the group's primary focus shifted to Barnes (Van Zant retired from the group in 2013).

Around mid-1976—between the time Ed King left Skynyrd and Steve Gaines came in—Carlisi attended rehearsals with Skynyrd. He even cowrote and played Dobro on "Four Walls of Raiford" with Ronnie Van Zant. It's not clear whether Van Zant intended to recruit Carlisi into Skynyrd, but Carlisi seemed like a logical choice—plus things weren't going very well for 38 Special at this point.

Many years later, after Carlisi left 38 Special in 1997, he stayed in Atlanta, where he worked with several groups, such as Big People, with Benjamin Orr on bass and vocals and Pat Travers on guitar, and Deep South with Ed King, Jimmy Hall and Robert Nix, and solo performer Brian Howe, who had earlier replaced Paul Rodgers in Bad Company. He said one of his favorite periods came when he worked with the Rock and Roll Hall of Fame Band alongside bassist Will Lee and drummer Liberty DeVitto, backing up singers like Ronnie Spector, Mitch Ryder, Patty Smyth and others. He also wrote a book, *Jam! Amp Your Team, Rock Your Business*, that was published in 2009. He now lives in St. Augustine.

Richard Donald Barnes grew up in the same Cedar Hills subdivision as Carlisi and Collins (along with Leon Wilkeson, Billy Powell and Kevin Elson), but Carlisi didn't get to know him until much later. Barnes's father was a music minister at a Baptist church. Barnes was introduced to playing music by way of piano lessons. He got his first electric guitar, a cheap Japanese Kingston, at the age of thirteen, and like Carlisi, he began pedaling his bicycle over to Collins's house to trade licks.[282] Like many, if not most, of the Westside players, Barnes, Carlisi and Collins, along with Dave Hlubek, were fans of Cream—hence, they were Clapton acolytes.

Not long after Barnes was caught in Donnie Van Zant's trailer, trying to steal a guitar, his parents sent him off to military school, which is probably where he gained a sense of discipline and organization. Upon returning home, he worked with local teen groups like the Six Teens, the Nu-Sounds and the Camelots. The latter group won a 1967 battle of the bands sponsored by the Jacksonville JayCees, beating out Donnie Van Zant's Sons of Satan, Doomsday Refreshment Committee (Carlisi was not yet in the band) and Rickey Medlocke's Miracle Sounds. The prize was four hours of studio time at Fuller Productions in Tampa.

Over the years it seems Barnes's guitar work has been overshadowed by his singing and by the fact that Carlisi played the solos on most of 38 Special's hits. However, Barnes played many solos on album cuts and on

PRIZES			
	10:30	CELLOPHANE FLOWER	REX CREEKMUR
400.00 RECORDING SESSION BY	10:45	THE MIRCLE SOUNDS	RICKEY MEDLOCK
FULLER PRODUCTIONS OF TAMPA	11:00	MULTIPLE SOUNDS INC.	PHILLIP CRAPSE
	11:15	SUNS OF SATAN	DONNIE VAN ZANT
	11:30	SOUND MUTATION	STEVE MOODY
MICROPHONE BY	11:45	THE NATURAL'S	WAYNE LOSCA
MARVIN KAY'S	12:00	DOOMSDAY REFRESHMENT COMM.	ROBERT CORCORAN
	12:15	THE INVICTAS	RONNIE EDENFIELD
	12:30	UNKNOWN	WILLIAM GILSDORF
	12:45	THE DISTORTIONS	MICHAEL KNEBEL
CLOTHES BY	1:00	THE AGENTS	NORMAN PAGANO
HALPERN'S	1:15	INVASIONS OF PSYCHEDELIC SOUNDS	RICK ERBY
	1:30	THE CAMELOTS	JOHN ROBBINS
	1:45	THE EPICS	DON BAKER
TROPHIES	2:00	THE MONARCHS	GLENN JACKSON
	2:15	THE CRYPTS	JERRY HAMPTON
	2:45	OUR GANG	RUSSELL GILBERT
	3:00	WE THE PEOPLE	DENNIS CONLIN
	3:15	THE BARONS	RICK POLAND
	3:30	THE CRESCENDOS	DENNIS OTT
	3:45	BLU-VISIONS IN-TYME	SPIKE LOUDERMILK
	8:30	THE TEN FINALISTS BEGIN	

Jacksonville Jaycees' Battle of the Bands listing, 1968. *Public domain.*

stage. "He's a really good player," Steve Wheeler said. "He's very precise and very soulful." Barnes always played his trademark Les Paul Jr., along with a double-cutaway Ibanez he keeps tuned in drop-D.[283]

Barnes left 38 Special in 1987 in an attempt to start a solo career. He returned after five years in the cold. These days he is the only original member of the group. In 2019, Barnes added renowned Atlanta guitarist Jerry Riggs to the lineup, which also includes St. Augustine bassist Barry Dunaway. Barnes lives in Marietta, outside Atlanta.

───────

THIRTY-EIGHT SPECIAL WAS NOT the only Jacksonville group that struggled to get out from under the southern-rock yoke.

The youngest Van Zant sibling, Johnny, started out as a drummer. He was only sixteen years old when Lynyrd Skynyrd suffered its historic plane crash, in which the eldest Van Zant brother, Ronnie, was killed. Johnny's other brother, Donnie, helped him get his act together as a singer, and he formed his own group, the Austin Nickels Band, that same year. He moved out front and brought in his nephew Robbie Morris on drums.

As mentioned earlier, in those days, a rock band was considered only as good as its guitarist(s), so Van Zant sought the best who were available. Fortunately, Jacksonville was loaded with excellent players. The first two guitarists he recruited were Marvin "Jet" Jarrett and Robbie Gay. Jarrett, who had been playing for only a couple of years at this point, left early on and was replaced by Erik Lundgren, a phenomenal young player from Jacksonville Beach who had studied under Robert Conti.

With a name change to the Johnny Van Zant Band, the group signed with Polydor Records in 1979—the same year Molly Hatchet went platinum with *Flirtin' with Disaster*—and a year later, the group released its debut album, *No More Dirty Deals*, supervised by former Skynyrd producer Al Kooper and recorded in Doraville at Studio One. But 1980 was not a good year to be launching a southern-rock group. The *Washington Post* branded the group's sound "southern boogie," which was "a declining commodity on the rock exchange." Music writer Mike Joyce went even further, stating:

> *Van Zant did nothing to advance the music....*[M]*any of his songs hardly seemed worth the effort....* "Statesboro Blues" *only reinforced the band's tradition-bound image. Guitarists Robbie Gay and Erik Lundgren didn't help matters. More often than not, they seemed content to echo the relationship between Skynyrd's Rossington and Collins.*[284]

Johnny Van Zant needed to update his sound and style. It took the group a couple of years to come to this realization, but by 1985, they were sounding more like Bon Jovi than Skynyrd. That was the year the group moved over to Vancouver-based Nettwerk Records, distributed by Geffen. Still, no hits ensued. Johnny fronted the Skynyrd reunion tour in 1987 but kept his band members on retainer until he finally decided to make Skynyrd his permanent priority. He also released a solo album, *Brickyard Road*, in 1990 for Atlantic Records, which made a small splash with a single and video of the same title.

Lundgren, whose playing has been compared to virtuosos such as Steve Vai and Joe Satriani, hung on to Johnny's coattails as long as he could— perhaps he was hoping Van Zant could bring him into Skynyrd. If he had been, he might have been the best guitarist Skynyrd ever had, technically speaking. But it didn't happen. Lundgren is also an impressive singer, far outshining Van Zant in both range and feel. In the early 1990s, Lundgren worked briefly with Molly Hatchet, alongside Bobby Ingram and former Wild Cherry guitarist Brian Bassett.

Lundgren returned to Jacksonville Beach and began performing in a duo with keyboardist-vocalist Bobby Capps, who had moved to Jacksonville from Arkansas and had done a stint with the Johnny Van Zant Band. Capps is now a keyboardist and singer with 38 Special.

Lundgren later worked with Johnny as well as Donnie Van Zant in a duo the brothers formed called, predictably, Van Zant. The duo signed with

Columbia Nashville, scoring two top-twenty country hits in 2005. But both Donnie and Johnny went back to their respective bands, 38 Special and Skynyrd, leaving Lundgren high and dry once again. Lundgren was—and is—certainly talented enough to work with any number of top-notch touring bands or even front his own, but major success has eluded him. He has also done some session work in Jacksonville studios and is currently working with his brother's group, the Paul Lundgren Band.

⚬⚭⚬

ANOTHER JACKSONVILLE GROUP THAT jumped on the southern-rock bandwagon in the 1970s, Blackfoot, was forced to jump back off in the 1980s. Two of that group's original members, Rickey Medlocke and Greg T. Walker, were Paxon High students and had worked together in a couple of teen bands. By 1969, Medlocke and Walker had added guitarist Charlie Hargrett, who had moved to Jacksonville with his family from Yonkers, New York, when he was fourteen, and they were calling themselves Fresh Garbage, after a song by California psychedelic group Spirit. With Medlocke on drums and vocals, Fresh Garbage did a stint at downtown Jacksonville's Comic Book Club, where such prominent Jacksonville groups like the Bitter Ind, One Percent (Lynyrd Skynyrd) and Daytona Beach's Allman Joys had served residencies.

Medlocke and Walker then joined Jacksonville guitarist Jerry Zambito's group, Tangerine, which was working Dub's Steer Room in nearby Gainesville with keyboardist DeWitt Gibbs and drummer Jakson Spires, who were also Paxon alumni. Zambito, who had helped the Mods win their 1966 battle of the bands (see chapter 3), was replaced by Hargrett, and Medlocke was selected as the frontman, whereupon the group changed its name to Hammer.[285]

In 1970, the members of Hammer made a trip to New York, where they had a connection in the Brill Building, and settled nearby in New Jersey. After a lot of scuffling and starving, nothing much happened. Medlocke returned to Jacksonville to play drums and sing with Lynyrd Skynyrd. Walker followed a little later, and Hammer was kaput.

However, Walker apparently did not feel fulfilled while working with Skynyrd and wanted to get Hammer—or a new version of it—back together.[286] "I was really missing Blackfoot and told Medlocke I wanted to get [Spires] and [Hargrett] back together and resume where we left off."[287]

RICK MEDLOCKE   JAKSON SPIRES   CHARLIE HARGRETT   GREG T. WALKER

BLACKFOOT

Blackfoot, circa 1979. Atco Records publicity photograph.

After some dilly-dallying, Medlocke went with him, and with the addition of guitarist Charlie Hargrett, along with Spires, Blackfoot was born.

The group started off with a heavier sound than that of Skynyrd's—you couldn't even call it southern rock, really—and soon landed a deal with Jimmy Johnson at Muscle Shoals Sound, with whom Medlocke and Walker had worked on Skynyrd's Muscle Shoals recordings.

In 1974, it seemed like everyone was jumping on the southern-rock bandwagon. However, even after landing album deals with Island Records and Epic/CBS, Blackfoot struggled in obscurity until signing with Ann Arbor–based manager and music-store owner Al Nalli in 1978. It just so happened that Nalli's sister was a vice-president at Atco Records in New York, which signed Blackfoot.

After years of struggle, things started looking up for Blackfoot. The group's first hit, "Highway Song," from its 1979 Atco album, *Blackfoot Strikes*, hewed to the "Free Bird" formula: a dirgy melody followed by an extended dual-lead solo in double-time. The group's second Atco single, "Train, Train," was far heavier, almost metal-ish, and probably would not have been described as southern rock had the group not been from Jacksonville.

Unfortunately, that train had already left the station. By 1980, southern rock was done. Thanks to MTV, how an act looked mattered as much as how it sounded. Blackfoot came under a lot of pressure from Atco to update its sound and look. Hargrett, who was follicularly challenged, caught much of the flak. The group brought in former Uriah Heep keyboarist Ken Hensley to add some synthesizers, which management thought might give the band a bit of a new-wave flavor. By appealing to a new audience, however, the group risked losing its core following, Walker said. He felt the group was selling out and unnecessarily so, because it was bound to lose its deal with Atco in any event.[288]

Guitarist Charlie Hargrett was the first to leave. Afterward, members came and went. By 1987, Medlocke was the only original member left, having secured the rights to the name Blackfoot after a lawsuit. At one point, Hargrett and Walker licensed the name from Medlocke. In 1996, Medlocke got a call from Gary Rossington, asking him if he'd like to rejoin Lynyrd Skynyrd, this time on guitar, playing Allen Collins's parts. That role had been filled from 1987 to 1994 by Randall Hall. Medlocke agreed, learned the parts faithfully and is still a member of the group at the time of this writing. However, he does not perform any lead vocals with the group, and it's a shame, because he's probably a better singer than guitarist.[289]

WHEN DANNY JOE BROWN left Molly Hatchet in 1980, he formed the Danny Joe Brown Band with his former Rum Creek cohort Bobby Ingram, who is the current leader of Molly Hatchet. They recruited Jacksonville guitarist Steve Wheeler, who did some writing for the group as well. Wheeler wrote the band's only hit single, "No One Walks on Me," which was released on Epic in 1981 and received rotation on MTV. Little did they know southern rock was on its way out, choking on its own excesses.

Born in Jacksonville, Wheeler had, like dozens of local boys, been inspired to take up the guitar after seeing the Beatles on the *Ed Sullivan Show*. His

Steve Wheeler, 2016. *Photograph by Frank Allen Sr.; used with permission.*

parents got him a cheap Winston acoustic, and his older brother had an Epiphone Caballero. "He taught me how to play 'House of the Rising Sun,'" Wheeler said.[290] Steve was nine years old when his older sister took him to the Jacksonville Coliseum to see the Monkees. "I had no idea who Jimi Hendrix was," Wheeler said, "but he changed my life."[291]

Wheeler was also inspired by local players like Sonny Faircloth and jazz great Robert Conti, the latter he took a few lessons from. He appreciated jazz and enjoyed Gary Starling's work as well. Another local player who impressed him was Jim Brown, who performed with prog-rock group Scepter. And of course, he was into big-name British players like Clapton, Beck, Page and Kossoff: "I modeled my vibrato after [Kossoff's]."[292] He also got into the southern-pickers like Duane Allman, Dickey Betts and Barry Bailey.

In 1979, Wheeler worked with Jacksonville's Bonnie Gringo, a southern-rock outfit formed by Indiana guitarist Tim Briggs and his brother David (Tim Briggs went on to become a touring member of the country group Alabama). After that, Wheeler formed Money with bassist Larry Steele (the author of the memoir *As I Recall*) and drummer Jimmy Dougherty, both of whom had been with popular psychedelic band Black Bear Angel.

When Danny Joe Brown left DJBB to return to Hatchet in 1982, the other members formed Vigil Annie and, for a time, did a bit of touring around the Southeast. It looked like Vigil Annie might be the next big group out of Jacksonville, but despite its strong musicianship, Vigil Annie fizzled quickly.

After an unproductive spell in Atlanta, Wheeler returned to Jacksonville to join Big Engine alongside former Hatchet bassist Banner Thomas—whom Wheeler said was also an excellent guitarist—along with other groups like All About Eve and Southern Rock Rebellion (with Charlie Hargrett from Blackfoot and Buzzy Meekins, formerly of the Outlaws and the DJBB).

In 2015, Wheeler and former Molly Hatchet drummer Bruce Crump joined a reconstituted edition of China Sky. The group's long-overdue follow-up was released by Britain's Escape Music. Wheeler now lives in Jacksonville.

China Sky, 2015. *Left to right*: Steve Wheeler, Ron Perry, Bruce Crump, Tim McGowan and Richard Smith. *Escape Music publicity photograph, by Ron Perry; used with permission.*

Bobby Ingram had been around for some time before joining Brown's solo band. He was born and raised in Jacksonville and began playing guitar at the age of eleven, later buying his first Gibson from Fred Paulus. His guitar hero was Allen Collins. It wasn't so much what Collins played, he said, but how he played it: "No one has the fire and feel that Allen had."[293]

Ingram grew up in the Arlington area, where he attended Terry Parker High School (class of 1975). His first band was called the Image, and "we were really quite bad," he said.[294] While attending junior college, Ingram formed Rum Creek, which included Danny Joe Brown as the lead singer (Brown was an insurance agent at the time). Brown left Rum Creek after about a year to join Hatchet. Another member of Rum Creek was Jacksonville guitarist Scott Montgomery, who later joined the new-wave group the Philters (led by guitarist-vocalist Phil Helow). Guitarist Mike Owings, who had worked with the Allen Collins Band as well as David Allan Coe, had also been a member. Owings praises Ingram's work: "Bobby is easily one of the best players in Jacksonville."[295]

In the mid-1980s, Ingram formed the Bobby Ingram Project, which briefly included singer Jimmy Dougherty. Ingram managed to snag an offer

Bobby Ingram with Molly Hatchet, circa 2017. *Courtesy of Bobby Ingram.*

from Pat Armstrong's PARC label, and Detroit singer-guitarist Ron Perry was brought aboard. The group changed its name to China Sky. All but three of the original players were let go by the powers that be; to make matters worse, Ingram got an offer to replace Molly Hatchet founder Dave Hlubek and was touring with that band for much of the time China Sky was recording its debut. He left China Sky just as its debut album was coming out. Instead of replacing him, the two remaining members, Perry and bassist Richard Smith, abandoned the project and retired to perform as a duo in Jacksonville Beach. Perry later formed his own band. In 2015 Perry and Smith reformed China Sky with Steve Wheeler and Bruce Crump.

Ingram stayed with Hatchet, and since 2000, when the last founding member, Duane Roland, sold him he rights to the name, has been the group's leader. He told interviewer Lisa Morgan that keeping Molly Hatchet on the treadmill is a labor of love: "I have always felt a need and strong desire to keep the Molly Hatchet tradition, legacy and spirit alive."[296]

⤞⤝

BARRY LEE HARWOOD CAME to Jacksonville as a toddler with his parents, a musical duo. Harwood himself is an impressive guitarist and an accomplished singer-songwriter. He also plays mandolin, Dobro, pedal steel and banjo. Chances are, if an instrument's got strings, Harwood can find his way around it.

His father, Clarence, played bass, and his mother played lap steel; from North Carolina, they brought their bluegrass and gospel to the *Glenn Reeves*

Show on WFGA (Channel 12), which was syndicated on fourteen other stations throughout the Southeast.[297] Harwood wanted to play bass, too, but his father bought him an acoustic guitar when he was very young and taught him mandolin at the age of fourteen.

Harwood told interviewer Scott Green he always knew he would make his career in music. "I never even thought about doing anything else."[298] He attended Arlington Junior High School, where he met future drummer Derek Hess while playing in the school band. Hess played saxophone; Harwood played clarinet. Like many Jacksonville musicians of the era, the Beatles inspired them to get into rock 'n' roll.[299] "Derek and some other guys had a band, and there was this talent show," Harwood told interviewer Scott Greene. "I went and saw them play, and when the girls went wild, I knew I wanted to be in that band. So I talked to Derek and ended up joining that band. We called ourselves the Rockers."[300] Harwood started out on bass in the Rockers but soon switched to guitar.[301]

In 1972, Harwood and Hess helped singer Maurice Samples form Christian-rock band Israel (Samples had a connection at Bell Records from his days with regional favorites Mouse and the Boys). Israel did some recording in Atlanta with producer Phil Gernhard; however, nothing much came from these sessions.

Impressed with Harwood's skills, Gernhard put him to work with Winter Haven singer Lobo (Kent LaVoie) and Jim Stafford, both major artists in the early 1970s. He also worked with Atlanta hitmaker Paul Davis. Harwood was in Atlanta in when Lynyrd Skynyrd needed some mandolin and Dobro on a song titled "Made in the Shade" for the group's 1975 album, *Nuthin' Fancy.*

Harwood went back to Jacksonville to join a new version of Randall Hall's group, Running Easy (with Derek Hess replacing Joe Kremp on drums). The members of that group—except for bassist-singer Gary Goddard—had been recruited by singer Melanie to go to Europe as her backing band. Harwood stayed on with her and even played on two of her albums. He was still working with her when Dean Kilpatrick, an assistant with Skynyrd, called and offered him Ed King's slot. "I had given my word that I would tour with Melanie," Harwood told Greene. He was hoping to work something out with Skynyrd when he got back, but by that point, the group had hired Steve Gaines.[302] He remained on good terms with the Skynyrd boys and played on 1976's "All I Can Do Is Write about It" (*Gimme Back My Bullets*) and 1977's "Honky-Tonk Nighttime Man" (*Street Survivors*, the group's last album before the plane crash).

In Orlando, he contributed tracks for Alias's 1979 debut for Mercury Records. That short-lived group featured singers Jimmy Dougherty and former Honkette JoJo Billingsley; other sidemen on the project included Skynyrd members Leon Wilkeson, Billy Powell and Artimus Pyle.

Ready to get back to work, Skynyrd guitarists Gary Rossington and Allen Collins formed the Rossington-Collins Band (RCB). They brought Harwood in as a third guitarist, singer and songwriter. Skynyrd drummer Artimus Pyle had broken his leg just as rehearsals were starting, so Harwood recommended Derek Hess as a replacement. Harwood cowrote and sang the RCB's breakthrough single, "Don't Misunderstand Me," alongside singer Dale Krantz, a former backup vocalist for 38 Special. The group's debut was held in 1980 at New Orleans's seventy-four-thousand-seat Superdome, and the RCB's debut album, *Anytime, Anyplace, Anywhere* was certified gold. Harwood wrote or cowrote three songs for that album and another four for their 1981 follow-up, *This Is the Way*.

Success brought its own peculiar pitfalls. Drug and alcohol abuse took an incredible toll on the group and its members. Even worse, Collins's wife had

Barry Harwood (*second from the left*) with the Rossington Collins Band, circa 1980. *MCA Records publicity photograph.*

died tragically, and Collins was going through a major meltdown. "When Allen's wife, Kathy, died, it broke his spirit," Harwood told Scott Greene. "We all knew it was over, and we all accepted it."[303]

In 1982, Rossington and Krantz, now an item, left the group—partly, they said, to get away from the drugs and the drama.[304] They later started their own group, the Rossington Band, signing with Atlantic Records in 1986. The other members of RCB, with the addition of Randall Hall, carried on as the Allen Collins Band (ACB), bringing in Jimmy Dougherty as the lead singer. Alas, the former Skynyrd members' luck had run out, and the ACB fizzled after only one album.

Exhausted and wrung out, Harwood went back to Jacksonville and got a day job.

> A lot of the substance abuse started in RCB, continued through ACB, and when it was all over, I was left alone with addiction demons to deal with....Drugs and alcohol caused me to miss opportunities. I went through the obligatory car crashes, hospitals, jail, suicide attempts and, of course, divorces.[305]

When Collins decided to put together a 1987 Lynyrd Skynyrd tribute tour commemorating the tenth anniversary of the plane crash, someone from the group contacted Harwood to offer him the slot as a third guitarist (Rossington and King were already on board). Harwood, trying to stay straight, had serious misgivings about climbing back on the party-go-round: "I knew if I took it [the offer], I would be right back where I was trying so hard to get away from."[306] The gig went to Randall Hall.

Staying put in Jacksonville, Harwood cobbled together a new group with former Hatchet guitarist Dave Hlubek. Drummer Scott Sisson, who worked with the Hlubek-Harwood Band, said Harwood is an excellent player, very melodic and consistent. In addition, "as a writer, he has a gift for melody."[307]

Harwood performed with a series of short-lived local bands for the next decade or two, including Time Piece and Little Maggie. He also played with the worship band at Jacksonville's New Life Christian Fellowship alongside former 38 Special drummer Jack Grondin. Harwood went to Nashville in the mid-2000s to try to put something together with Ed King, but that project never got off the ground. In 2010—thirty years after his success with the RCB—Harwood went back to his gospel and bluegrass roots, issuing an independently released album, *Southern Part of Heaven*, for which he wrote ten out of eleven songs. He now lives in Nashville.

BY THE LATE 1980s, southern-rock had become a tired joke among Jacksonville musicians. Yet this was exactly the point when Allen Collins—already debilitated by an automobile accident—decided to put Lynyrd Skynyrd back together. Collins had known Randall Hall since Running Easy opened for Skynyrd at Friendship Park back in 1972.

Hall's early guitar heroes included the triumvirate of Clapton, Beck and Page, along with Hendrix, Johnny Winter and Mike Bloomfield. He learned of Bloomfield from Al Kooper's 1968 album *Super Session*, which featured guitarists Bloomfield, Al Kooper and Stephen Stills letting loose on some long jams.

The members of Running Easy had been pals with the Skynyrd boys, even sharing a rehearsal space near Green Cove Springs they called "Hell House."[308] Ronnie Van Zant touted Hall's talents to all who would listen and gave him career advice. Hall was working as a yard-maintenance man at a Westside apartment complex when Van Zant happened to drive by. Hall told Michael Buffalo Smith, "I was digging a hole with filth and dirt all over me, and [Ronnie pulled up and] said, 'Randall, what the hell are you doing?' I said, 'I'm digging a hole.' He said, 'Man, you're too good to be doing this shit.'"[309]

Running Easy also included left-handed guitar phenom Jim Harrison, one of Hall's favorite local players who went on to record a single for Capitol with Page Matherson's group Richfield. Hall retained the Running Easy name while basically forming a new group, which briefly included Harwood on guitar and vocals. The new edition of Running Easy also included Derek Hess, bassist-vocalist Gary Goddard and keyboardist Steve Perez.

Hall was considered for a spot with the Rossington-Collins Band in 1979 but was beat out by Harwood, because Harwood sang more and wrote lots of songs.[310] Hall was working with local bar band the Moody Brothers when he was recruited into the Allen Collins Band. Collins retained Harwood on guitar and vocals, adding Hall to the mix along with frontman Jimmy Dougherty, who had also been working with the Moody Brothers, as a drummer and singer.[311] The Allen Collins Band, formed in 1983, enjoyed a strong lineup, but it didn't last. The main problem was that Collins went off the rails; not only that, the band had also lost its staunchest supporters at MCA in a corporate restructuring.

Southern rock had been expired for some time when the ACB fizzled. Hall went back to working with local bands. By 1987, he was working six nights a week with Synergy, a Jacksonville Beach bar band, when he got another

Allen Collins Band, 1983. Randall Hall (*left*). *MCA Records publicity photograph.*

call from Collins (after Harwood had turned him down). Hall went out with the Skynyrd "tribute tour" that year and became a full-time member when the group signed with Atlantic Records in 1990. Ed King was brought back as well, and he and Hall worked side by side. Hall played on three albums with Skynyrd: *Southern by the Grace of God, Lynyrd Skynyrd 1991* and *The Last Rebel.* The powers that be decided Hall was making too much money as a principal and proposed converting his status to that of a salaried sideman. Hall refused, a lawsuit ensued and he settled out of court in 2000 for an undisclosed sum.[312]

He formed the Randall Hall Band with Dougherty on drums and Tim Lindsey (now with Molly Hatchet) on bass. At times, the group also performed as the Artimus Pyle Band with the former Skynyrd drummer.[313] Hall is still working, performing regularly with World Class Rockers.

9

BEYOND SOUTHERN ROCK

Southern rock had come and gone, but Jacksonville's music scene refused to die.

John Kurzweg lived in Jacksonville for only about a year, but he left a major impression. Local guitarists used to joke, "He's making us look bad—we're gonna have to break a couple of his fingers or something."

Drummer Scott Sisson, who briefly worked with Kurzweg, said Kurzweg had his own vocabulary on guitar. "He didn't play the blues-based stuff most of the players around here did."[314] Randall Hall, who also worked with him in Synergy, agreed: "He was definitely from a different school."[315]

Born in San Francisco, the son of a Lutheran minister, Kurzweg moved around the country with his family. While living in Richmond, Kurzweg played the flute in a school band and had taken piano lessons as a kid. He started studying the guitar with jazz player Jerry Fields. "I started to figure out my own version of music theory and mixed that with what [my instructors had] taught me."[316] His other influences were Mark Farner, Joe Walsh and Carlos Santana.[317] As good as he was as a guitarist, he became most successful with his singing. His local hero was guitarist Steve Taff, who was a few years older, and he would later work with him in the Tallahassee group Slapstick.[318]

Kurzweg first heard Lynyrd Skynyrd when he moved to Tallahassee in 1974. He liked all three of the group's guitarists, he said, but Ed King was the one who really fired his imagination. "He's a genius. His solos are just crazy." In Tallahassee, he worked with and fronted several local bands, including the Night, which became a fixture on the southeastern bar-band circuit in the early 1980s.[319]

After the Night broke up, Kurzweg bought a little four-track recorder, started making demos and gave a cassette tape to Kris Wrech, an acquaintance who had worked at University of Florida's Student Government Productions. Wrech had landed a job in New York at Atlantic Records and passed Kurzweg's tape to A&R man Frankie LaRocka. Kurzweg also attracted the attention of Pat Armstrong in Orlando, who offered to sign him to his PARC label.

After signing with Atlantic, Kurzweg recorded much of his 1987 debut album, *Wait for the Night*, at Bear Tracks Studio in Suffern, New York, with famed British producer-engineer Ken Scott at the helm.[320] Kurzweg became dissatisfied with the direction the album was taking—and his managers became alarmed at how little progress was being made—so he fired Scott and finished the album at Starke Lake Studio in Orlando, with engineer Dana Cornock coproducing.[321]

The album had gone way over budget, so when it came time to put a band together to tour behind it, Atlantic refused to advance tour-support funds to subsidize the band members' salaries.

Kurzweg came to Jacksonville in 1987. Lex Staley at FM station Rock 105 (WFYV-FM) had been playing his song "What's It Gonna Be." Kurzweg's relations with Atlantic were in the toilet. He abandoned the album project to join Jacksonville Beach bar band Synergy, which included Randall Hall and drummer Derek Hess. "Playing alongside Randall made me up my game," Kurzweg said. Other Jacksonville players he admired were Rocco Marshall, also with Synergy, and Roosters members Billy Bowers, Gary Smalley and Steve Shanholzer.

Being aware of—and inspired by—the fierce competition among guitarists in the area, Kurzweg worked to not only improve his playing but also distinguish himself from others, many of whom were recycling the same tired licks. "I found my own voice [on guitar] while living in Jacksonville."[322]

He returned to Tallahassee to put together a studio in a rented house, where he began engineering and producing recordings for area acts like House of Dreams, the Sight-Seers and newcomers Creed. The latter group snagged a major-label deal and scored platinum in 1997. Kurzweg, virtually a fifth member of Creed, oversaw the group's arrangements, sang backgrounds and played keyboards for several of its recordings.[323]

Kurzweg later produced Puddle of Mudd's debut album for Fred Durst's Flawless label—sales of which hit three million. Other acts he worked with

John Kurzweg, 2018. *Photograph by Katherine St. John; used with permission.*

included Godsmack, Eagle-Eye Cherry, Jewel and Big Head Todd & the Monsters—altogether racking up a sales volume of forty million or more units. He now lives in Santa Fe, New Mexico, where he operates a private production studio.

THE LATE 1980s SPAWNED something of a rock renaissance in Jacksonville; power trio Rein Sanction was part of that revival. Fronted by guitarist Mark Gentry, who played a combination of rhythm and lead, Rein Sanction materialized on the local scene sometime around 1987.

Gentry's style was angular, aggressive and noisy, reminiscent of New York's "no wave" movement of the late 1970s. His guitar work also contained echoes of Hendrix's style at its most unhinged, blended with the frantic intensity of Neil Young's playing.[324] Scott Sisson, who played a couple of dates with Gentry, thought he was trying to make his guitar sound like a different instrument: "I didn't know what he was going for, but it wasn't guitar."[325]

REIN SANCTION

Rein Sanction, 1991.
Left to right: Ian Chase,
Brannon Gentry and
Mark Gentry. *Sub Pop
Records publicity photograph.*

Rein Sanction included Mark's brother, Brannon Gentry, on drums and his neighbor Ian Chase on bass, who is himself also no slouch on guitar.[326] Chase said Mark Gentry was a tortured soul who was able to evoke his dark emotions on the guitar. His other influences, he said, were Joy Division and the Athens, Georgia group Pylon.[327] Bradley Torreano of *AllMusic* described the band's sound as "the same brand of sludge-pop" as Dinosaur Jr., and the group would be hounded by this comparison.[328] Rein Sanction was also influenced by 1960s acid rockers Blue Cheer, as evidenced by its version of "Summertime Blues," which was included in the group's live set.[329]

By 1989, Rein Sanction had released a seven-song, self-titled EP that was recorded in Gainesville at Mirror Image Studio. After some initial interest from British label Rough Trade, the group signed with Seattle's Sub Pop Records in 1991, releasing the album *Broc's Cabin*, followed a year later by *Mariposa*, which included a remake of an obscure Hendrix tune, "Aint No Telling."

The group, however, was beset by problems—not the least of which was poor sales—and imploded in 1993, after a disastrous tour. "It was one continuous disaster," Chase said.[330]

Regrouping thirteen years later under the name Mark Gentry and Rein Sanction, with new bassist Darren Bedford, the band released a three-song EP with Seattle's Flotation Records, to no great acclaim. The group continued to play shows around Jacksonville. Southern Lord Records rereleased its debut EP in 2019, and the group released an acoustic-laden collection via Bandcamp in 2021. Mark Gentry's guitar work has gotten more bluesy and noticeably subdued. The Gentry brothers now live in Dickson, Tennessee, where they perform occasionally.[331]

DEREK TRUCKS IS ON the short list of the most important and highly respected players who came out of Jacksonville.

Born in the city in 1979, he is the nephew of Allman Brothers Band drummer Butch Trucks. His father, Chris, a roofer, played acoustic guitar; young Derek took an interest in the instrument around the age of eight. Chris Trucks said, "Everything I know, he learned in thirty minutes."[332]

Derek began taking lessons from Jim Graves, a prominent local player, and learned to play the slide guitar from Steve Wheeler.[333] He told interviewer Rick Beato that the starting point for slide players is the work of Elmore James. He also studied Charlie Patton and Bukka White. He cites Johnny Winter, Lowell George and Jesse Ed Davis as major influences. "I think of it [slide guitar] as a human voice," he told Beato.[334]

One of the main reasons he took up the slide was that his hands were so small.[335] Soon his father began taking him around town to sit in with local bands like the Greg Baril Band and Ace Moreland's Westside Story. He became a semiregular performer on Sunday afternoons at the Crab

Derek Trucks (*left*) with the Greg Baril Band. Crab Pot, Jacksonville Beach, circa 1989. *Photograph by Lisa Collins; used with permission.*

Pot restaurant in Jacksonville Beach. He was a little towhead, with an SG Standard that was almost as big as he was.

Guitarist Greg Baril, a hotshot in his own right, soon realized the kid could draw audiences. The Greg Baril Band, with the addition of keyboardist Mike Hollingsworth, became the Derek Trucks Band.

Trucks began sitting in with acts all over the Southeast, including his uncle's group, the Allman Brothers Band. At a date in South Miami Beach, Gregg Allman gave Derek a slide that had belonged to Duane Allman.[336] He also sat in with Eric Clapton, Joe Walsh, Stephen Stills, Buddy Guy and Bob Dylan. In the early 1990s, singer-guitarist Danny Roberts and drummer Derek Hess became members of his band.

Trucks then went to Atlanta to form a new group, and the Derek Trucks Band released its debut album with Landslide Records (owned by former Jacksonville resident Michael Rothschild) in 1997. He was made a full-time member of the ABB in 1999 while continuing to perform with his own group in his off time. The Derek Trucks Band's eighth album, *Already Free*, released by Sony's Legacy division, won a Grammy award in 2010 for Best Contemporary Blues Album.

That same year, Trucks and his new wife, Susan Tedeschi, pooled their resources and formed the Tedeschi Trucks Band, which has since been recording and touring steadily, having released several albums, most of which were recorded at a studio on the couple's property near Julington Creek.

Trucks is often considered southern-rock royalty; his music leans heavily on the blues and R&B, with a taste of jazz, as did the ABB's early work. He has never had what one might call a hit record, but he has a steady following who will pretty much accept whatever he wants to release. He has even recorded a couple of John Coltrane tunes. He was named among the top 100 guitarists of all time by *Rolling Stone* in 2011.

John Kurzweg had the opportunity to work with Trucks when he was producing an album for the Tallahassee band Uptown Rudy. The group recruited Trucks to play on a song called "Hillbilly Wine." As a player, Trucks is in a league of his own: "He's beyond everyone," Kurzweg said. "He's on a whole different level."[337]

Susan Tedeschi came to Jacksonville in 1999 to live with Derek Trucks, whom she met that year while her band was opening for the Allman Brothers Band in New Orleans. She was born in Boston, where she put together her first band in 1988 at the age of eighteen. After graduating from Berklee College of Music in 1991, she continued playing gigs around the Boston area. In 1995, Boston-based Oarfin Records released

Susan Tedeschi **Tone-Cool Records**
One Camp Street
Cambridge, MA 02140
(617) 354-0700
tonecool@tonecool.com
www.tonecool.com

Susan Tedeschi, circa 1998. *Tone-Cool Records publicity photograph, by Ron Powell.*

her debut album, *Better Days*, for which she wrote several songs and played rhythm guitar. She played lead guitar on one song and the slide guitar on a couple others. She was picked up by Boston's Tone-Cool Records, which released her second album, 1998's *Just Won't Burn*, which featured Atlanta hotshot Sean Costello on lead guitar. That album sold a whopping six hundred thousand copies, putting her indelibly on the musical map. She released more solo albums—two with Verve and one with New West—through 2008.

Tedeschi is best known for her powerhouse vocal style, which echoes the styles of Bonnie Raitt, Janis Joplin, Dale Krantz, Little Richard and Buddy Guy. She has mastered the blues-rock style and, as a singer, has few peers. Her guitar skills are modest but effective. She can lay down a good groove on rhythm, and her timing is rock-solid. Her soloing is good for the most part but lacks fluidity. She does, however, evince a distinct emotive style and manages to turn her lack of finesse into an advantage with the kind of jagged edge that has been used to great effect by the likes of Keith Richards, Duane Allman and Jimmy Page. Steve Wheeler, who has jammed with her, said, "She sounds like an authentic blues player—she's got that edge."[338]

Tedeschi and Trucks were married in 2001, and the couple has two children. They gave up their own bands in 2010 to create the Tedeschi Trucks Band (TTB), which stays busy on the road and makes records in their own studio. Trucks's mother looks after the couple's kids while they are on tour.[339] In 2019, the TTB released a live rendition of Eric Clapton's album *Layla*.

THE BIGGEST SIGNING SINCE Skynyrd occurred in 1996, with a rap-metal group called Limp Bizkit, led by singer-rapper Fred Durst. Durst came to Jacksonville from North Carolina in the early 1990s and formed Limp Bizkit with guitarist Wes Borland, a Douglas Anderson School of the Arts graduate who moved to Jacksonville with his parents from Richmond.

Just before a trip to Los Angeles to meet with label execs at MCA-distributed Mojo Records, Borland left the group and was briefly replaced by Jacksonville guitarist Terry Balsamo. Bizkit had a falling out with Mojo executives, went back to Jacksonville and then signed with New York–based Flip Records (distributed by Interscope). With Borland added back to the lineup, the group scored a hit with a rap-metal rendition of George Michael's "Faith." Limp Bizkit's follow-up album sold more than six million copies, and its third sold more than eight million.

Borland became known for not only his innovative guitar work but also his outrageous costumes and makeup. "I'm a comedian onstage," he said. Some of his schtick is inspired by professional wrestling.[340] Nonetheless, he knows what he's doing on guitar. "Borland is actually an incredibly talented musician," wrote reviewer Mark Urban, "and if you listen to a few Limp Bizkit tracks, you can actually hear a lot of great riffs."[341] Many of Limp Bizkit's songs are built around Borland's riffs.

Borland has also been known to stretch the capabilities of the guitar itself, sometimes playing a Yamaha seven-string (with a low B), as well as a Paul Reed Smith custom four-string using a peculiar tuning, which he used on the Limp Bizkit song "Nookie." He got the latter idea from Les Claypool of Primus.[342] Claypool has been a major influence for Borland.[343]

Steve Wheeler said Borland doesn't have amazing technique, but what he plays is tasteful and fits Limp Bizkit's overall aesthetic.[344]

Borland admitted, "I'm just not a fast player. I can't out-solo anyone, but I definitely can out-riff them, I think." A review of Limp Bizkit's recent album *Limp Bizkit Still Sucks*, released in 2021 with Suretone Records, stated:

> [Borland's] *eclectic riff wizardry remains as intriguing as ever, though he is unfortunately a bit reined in on many of the tracks featured here. The opener "Out of Style" does still manage to deliver a particularly nasty concoction of his wares though, with dive-bomb screeches and crunchy bounce grooves providing explosive sonic shrapnel.*[345]

One quality Borland shares with many Jacksonville musicians is his tremendous work ethic. He is nothing if not prolific, constantly creating new projects under various names. In 2001, he formed a side project called Big Dumb Face, which released an album with Durst's Flawless label (distributed by Interscope) in 2001. That same year, he and his brother Scott Borland, Limp Bizkit's's keyboardist, left the band to form a short-lived group called Eat the Day with former Filter singer Richard Patrick.[346] Another project

The Three Headed Dimetrian Pup / The Tongue of Colicab / Joe Couch / The Cardboard Urinal

Big Dumb Face. Wes Borland (*left*). *Geffen Records publicity photograph, by Dave Gould.*

he created with his brother was Goatslayer. Borland also perfomed a nine-month stint with Marilyn Manson, during which he and the singer got into a scrap: "He tried to choke me out onstage, and I flipped him over and knocked the breath out of him."[347] Borland also served a short stint with Nine Inch Nails.

After a brief reunion with Limp Bizkit in 2004, Borland left the group again and formed Black Lights Burn, signing to former Limp Bizkit producer Ross Robinson's label, IAM: Wolfpack. He also spent a year as a bassist with a Robinson-produced group called From First to Last. Borland returned to Limp Bizkit a year later and has since been touring, albeit sporadically, with the group. During another Limp Bizkit hiatus, he performed with Queen Kwong, fronted by his then-wife, Carré Callaway (they divorced in 2019).

Borland has also dabbled in film scoring, mostly for horror movies. "I just love horror movies," he said.[348] He also hosts a podcast, *Space Zebra*, four times a week on Twitch. He now lives in Los Angeles, where he runs his own label, Edison Records.

After a short stint with Limp Bizkit in 1996, guitarist Terry Balsamo joined Jacksonville rock band Cold (formerly Grundig), which signed with Durst's Flawless label. Balsamo was with that group from 1999 to 2004. He later joined Arkansas-based rock band Evanescence, for which Cold had served as opening act. In 2015, Balsamo left Evanescence, rejoining Cold a year later. He left Cold again in 2018. He worked with Evanescence again in 2019.

⬥

POP-PUNK BAND YELLOWCARD, LED by guitarist Ben Harper, a former Douglas Anderson student, was formed in 1997. After appearing on a couple of indie labels, the group signed with Capitol in 2003 and had a huge hit with the album *Ocean Avenue*, which sold more than two million copies. Yellowcard's second Capitol album went gold (selling five hundred thousand units). In 2005, after leaving the group he founded, Harper decided to focus on his label, Takeover Records. He briefly worked with rock band Amber Pacific in 2006 and then with HeyMike! from 2009 to 2011. In 2014, Harper and original Yellowcard drummer Longineu Parsons III formed a new group called This Legend. He now lives in Long Beach, California.

Paul Phillips was born in Brunswick, Georgia, about seventy miles north of Jacksonville. His father was a guitarist in a local bar band. He started playing guitar around the age of eleven and got his first electric guitar, a Squier Stratocaster, at the age of fifteen. His early influences were Slash from Guns 'N' Roses, Dimebag Darrell of Pantera, Kirk Hammett of Metallica and Tony Iommi of Black Sabbath.[349]

While he was a student at the University of North Florida, he formed punk-ska band Happy Hour, of which former Jacksonville resident Fred Durst became a fan. Durst offered the group a deal with his Flawless label. Phillips dropped out of college to take advantage of the opportunity, but Durst didn't provide enough money for the members to live on. "We finally get the contract," he said at a 2015 panel discussion. "It [gave us] an advance of about $4,000. We had eight people—do the math. We weren't eating well."[350] Happy Hour imploded before they even got into the studio.

Phillips got another call from Durst in 2001, inviting him to audition for rock band Puddle of Mudd, which was already signed to Flawless. Phillips stayed with that group for about five years, appearing on two of its best-selling albums, *Come Clean* (2001), which sold three million units, and *Life on Display* (2003), which sold approximately five hundred thousand copies. Both albums were produced by onetime Jacksonville guitarist John Kurzweg.

Puddle of Mudd was very much a grunge band—a genre that eschewed rock excesses, such as guitar solos—in the vein of Nirvana, so there weren't many solos to be played. Phillips generally played either crunchy power chords or octave licks that functioned like horn lines, which is fitting, since he was a trained horn player. It might be safe to assume that he was not steeped in the standard blues-rock vernacular like many, if not all, Jacksonville players.

Kurzweg, who produced two albums for Puddle of Mudd, said Phillips could solo if he wanted to, but generally, "he was good at coming up with alternate melodies, little [decorative] parts to keep your interest in the song going." Phillips always worked out his parts in advance and generally did not improvise, Kurzweg said.[351]

In 2007, Phillips left Puddle of Mudd and joined Los Angeles–based metal band Operator, recording an album with Atlantic Records that year. He rejoined Puddle of Mudd in 2009, staying for another two years. He has also performed with Jacksonville-based rock band Society Red, alongside singer Damien Starkey and second guitarist Adam Latiff, both onetime members of Puddle of Mudd. He also tried his hand at acting, appearing in a 2013 short film, *The Guy Knows Everything*. Phillips, who still lives in Jacksonville, did a short stint as a DJ on the Brunswick, Georgia FM station Fox 107.7.

JOSH BURKE WAS SIXTEEN when he crashed a soundcheck of his favorite band, Red Jumpsuit Apparatus (RJA). The Middleburg, Florida group, whose 2006 debut with Virgin Records sold five hundred thousand units, was playing at a club in Syracuse, near Burke's hometown of Cicero, New York. Burke introduced himself and made a big impression on lead singer and rhythm guitarist Ronnie Winter.

Burke already knew several of Red Jumpsuit Apparatus's songs. He had taken up the guitar, a fifty-dollar Johnson model his father bought him, when he was eleven and began taking lessons at thirteen. "He's a quick learner," said Jimmy Falco, his teacher. "He's attached to the guitar. He sleeps with it."[352]

At the soundcheck, Burke offered to drive Winter to the local Guitar Center to pick up some strings. Winter asked the kid to grab a guitar and play something for him, so he did. "I was blown away," Winter said. With Josh's parents' permission, Winter took him to Florida for few days, two of which they spent in the band's Middleburg studio making demos of new songs.[353] Burke joined Red Jumpsuit Apparatus a year later as its lead guitarist, replacing Duke Kitchens and Matt Carter, who wanted to get off the road.[354]

Burke is clearly from the Eddie Van Halen "neoclassical" school. Randy Rhoads (of Quiet Riot and Blizzard of Oz) is also a big influence of his.[355] Burke has, to date, played on two Red Jumpsuit Apparatus EPs, *Et Tu, Brute* and *The Emergency*, along with two albums, *Four* and *The Awakening*. He also contributes as a cowriter.

Burke lives in Orange Park when he's not on the road. Like members of many groups, such as those of the Grateful Dead and the Allman Brothers Band, RJA's members have discovered that you don't need a hit record to build a following; it can be done the old-fashioned way—through nonstop touring and word of mouth.[356]

BEFORE JOINING SHINEDOWN, GUITARIST Jasin Todd was working with the Jacksonville death-metal band Nefarian, formed in 1994. In 2001, he was invited to join Shinedown, led by Knoxville, Tennessee singer Brent Smith, who already had a deal with Atlantic Records. Shinedown was basically formed at Judy Van Zant Jenness's Jacksonville Beach recording studio, Made in the Shade, with help from engineer Pete Thornton, who recruited musicians for the group. Todd also happened to be engaged to Van Zant's daughter, Melody.[357]

He recorded three albums with Shinedown, including the group's 2004 platinum breakthrough album, *Leave a Whisper*, which included an "unplugged" version of Lynyrd Skynyrd's "Simple Man," a tribute to Ronnie Van Zant. Todd left the group in 2008.

In 2010, Todd worked with Epic Records' act Fuel. In 2014, he toured Eastern Europe and South America with a revue called the Metal Allstars. That same year, he began working with Birmingham, Alabama metal band Maylene and the Sons of Disaster, but that band's schedule was derailed by injuries incurred by its lead singer. Todd appeared in Nashville with members of Slipknot and Havok at 2016's "Metal Fest: A Tribute to Roadrunner Records," performing a couple of numbers by the group Sepultura. He now lives in Nashville.

10

UP-AND-COMERS

Dylan Adams moved to Jacksonville from Tallahassee with his family when he was eight. He started playing guitar, an acoustic purchased from Walmart, about a year later. Within a few weeks, a cousin of his gave him a Peavey Strat copy. His first guitar hero was Angus Young of AC/DC.

Adams changed directions when heard his father playing the Allman Brothers Band's *Fillmore East* album. It was a revelation, he said. "That album sent me down the path I've gone on—traditional blues, R&B, soul and jazz," all of which he puts to use in local band Smokestack. The old-school stuff is the real deal, he said: "It's getting more common among people my age." The electric guitar seems to be making a comeback, he added: "There's a ton of new players coming up, and a lot of people are digging it."[358]

He's also a Skynyrd fan, especially of Steve Gaines, and admires Jeff Carlisi's work with 38 Special. Then there's the elephant in the room: Derek Trucks. "You can't talk about Jacksonville guitarists without mentioning him."[359]

Adams has written a few tunes of his own, mostly jazzy, jam-band stuff, he said. He now lives in Jacksonville Beach.

Steven Honig was born and raised in Jacksonville. His took an interest in music around the age of eight, so his parents got him piano lessons. At twelve, he decided to get into guitar, starting off on an acoustic, a Samick three-quarter scale—his parents didn't want an electric guitar in the house, he said. A year later, his uncle gave him a 1978 Hondo Revival (an Explorer knockoff). "I loved that thing," he said. His early guitar heroes were Page, Hendrix and Richie Blackmore. "They were the reason I wanted to play."

His first professional instrument was a Gibson SG, which he still owns. He was later inspired by Derek Trucks, who also favors an SG. "[Trucks's playing] hit me like a ton of bricks." Honig doesn't play slide guitar, but he does try to emulate slide licks.[360]

He played his first gig at Freebird Café, which was owned by Judy Jenness, Ronnie Van Zant's widow, and her daughter, Melody. His first band was called S.P.O.R.E. and was formed around 2012; he still works with them. He currently plays in four bands—all of which perform only originals—including neo-southern rockers Cowford, which he joined in 2015. Honig cuts a dashing figure with that group, with the look and appeal of a classic rock star.

The group Cowford came to the attention of Skynyrd keyboardist Peter Keys, who brought its players to Nashville in 2018 to record a four-song EP, *Swamp Songs*, at Sound Kitchen. Keys also contributed on the keyboards.[361]

Cowford is making some new recordings at Jacksonville's Pine Studios and is changing its style a bit, Honig said. Honig writes a good deal of Cowford's music, mainly coming up with riffs and chord progressions for which singer and rhythm guitarist Nat Spaulding Jr. writes toplines (lyrics and melodies). Although he is keeping his day job for the time being, he is grateful that he gets to play music for approving audiences. "I'm lucky I get to do this." He now lives in the Southside.

Born and raised in Orange Park, Buddy Crump began playing guitar at nine. His dad knew many musicians, so he was aware of Jacksonville's guitar-playing tradition from an early age, and this inspired him.

His first guitar was an acoustic; his first electric was an Epiphone Les Paul. His heroes were British players such as Clapton, Beck, Kossoff, Alvin Lee and Mick Ralphs, along with Americans Hendrix, Stevie Ray Vaughn, Joe Perry and Allen Collins.

He performed in his first live appearance at eleven, sitting in at Whitey's Fish Camp with with Rick Doeschler's group, the Bold City Band. At sixteen, he joined a Skynyrd tribute band called Pronounced in which he met guitarist-vocalist Ivan Pulley. Crump played "Free Bird" note for note and even bought a Firebird like Allen Collins's. This led to his garnering a steady gig with the Ivan Pulley Band in 2017.

In 2019, Crump helped form straight-ahead rock group Danger Bird—now called Fortune Child—which attracted the attention of producer-sound mixer Kevin Elson (whose credits include Lynyrd Skynyrd, Johnny Van Zant Band, Journey, Mr. Big and more). The group put down tracks at Jimmy DeVito's Retrophonics Studio in Crescent Beach. Elson came in to mix Fortune Child's independently released album, *Close to the Sun*.

Buddy Crump onstage with Fortune Child. *Photograph by Steve Boatwright; courtesy of Buddy Crump.*

Elson said Crump was definitely an old-school, British-style player. "He can shred," Elson said, "but I told him to keep it simple and play something people can hum [along with]." Elson also advised Crump that just because he's from Jacksonville, he shouldn't get locked into playing southern rock. Elson said he is trying to help take the group to the next level.[362]

Steve Wheeler said Crump is "a feel player [as opposed to a schooled player]. I like that."[363]

ACKNOWLEDGEMENTS

- My wife, Kirana Pinjai, for her unwavering belief and support.
- Joe Gartrell and the staff at The History Press for their support and enthusiasm.
- Mark Kohl for helping me hash out the theme of this book.
- Patrick Keeney for proofreading, suggestions and encouragement.
- Todd Roobin for his continued support and encouragement.
- Joe Kremp for inside information.
- Rick Doeschler for inside information.
- Walter Eaton for inside information.
- Derek Hess for inside information.
- Richard Mathews for inside information.
- Tom Markham for inside information.
- Allen Collins for inside information.
- Randall Hall for insight, comments and inside information.
- Jimmy Amerson for insight, comments and inside information.
- Auburn "Sam" Burrell for insight, comments and inside information.
- Steve Wheeler for insight, comments and inside information.
- Page Matherson for insight, comments and inside information.
- Scott Sisson for insight, comments and inside information.
- Jim Graves for insight and comments.
- David Rolland at the *Jitney* for his support.

- Jeff Carlisi for his photographs, comments and inside information.
- Larry Steele for keeping the memories.
- Gary Powell for his support and encouragement.
- Steve Reynolds for his support and encouragement.
- Paul Glass for showing me the secrets.
- Marion "Sister" Van Zant for her kindness and friendship.
- Leon Wilkeson for his friendship and photographs.
- Mary Wilkeson for her friendship and photographs.
- Gail Grimm Gerdes for photographs.
- Theresa Askins Steele for photographs.
- Red Slater for photographs.
- Michael Buffalo Smith for his hard work over the years and for his friendship and support.
- Scott B. Bomar for a kick-ass blurb.
- Rob Duner-Fenter for conceptual assistance.

NOTES

Preface

1. Page Matherson, telephone interview with author, June 24, 2022.
2. About $4,778.68 in 2022. CPI Inflation Calculator.
3. Aledort, "King Albert." I was not aware at the time that some blues guitarists, such as Albert King—who was one of Clapton's idols—tuned their guitars down to make string pulling easier.
4. Poe, *Skydog*, 70–71.
5. Facebook, "Florida Garage Bands." Wally Steinhauser, a Jacksonville musician whose father managed three city youth centers, including Woodstock, was able to put a date to this show, March 14, 1969, as well as a ticket price.
6. Price would go on to enjoy a distinguished career in Nashville, working with the likes of Lucinda Williams and Billy Joe Shaver.
7. ProSoundWeb, "In Profile: Veteran Mix Engineer Kevin Elson & His Work on the Current Kelly Clarkson Tour," February 10, 2010, https:// www.prosoundweb.com/in-profile-veteran-mix-engineer-kevin-elson- his-work-on-the-current-kelly-clarkson-tour/. Keyboardist/guitarist Kevin Elson would become a sound man/roadie for Lynyrd Skynyrd. He coproduced, along with engineer Rodney Mills at Studio One, one of Skynyrd's best albums, *Street Survivors* (parts of which were recorded in Miami at Criteria). After Skynyrd's 1977 plane crash, which he

was involved in, he joined Journey as the group's live sound mixer and became its studio engineer and producer. He produced some of Journey's best-selling albums, along with albums by Europe, Mr. Big and the Johnny Van Zant Band.

Introduction

8. Dunne, "Does It Have to Be So Loud?" 6.
9. Ibid.
10. Cartwright, "Kithara."
11. Newman, "History, Music and Instruments."
12. Wardlow and Komara, *Chasin' that Devil Music*, 196–97.
13. Worl, "What Sex?"
14. Hynde, *Reckless*, 52.
15. McMahan, "Don't Be That Guy."
16. *Reverbnation Blog*, "Electric Guitar's Decline"; see also Dunne, "Does It Have to Be So Loud?" 3.
17. Beato, "Rock Music?" In 2020 Gates, who is from Southern California, was named one of the best guitarists of the decade (2010–2019) by *Guitar World* magazine. *Guitar World*, "One Hundred Greatest Guitarists of All Time."
18. Eric Clapton, quoted in Williams, "Guitars Are Back."

Chapter 1

19. I am being somewhat—though not entirely—facetious here.
20. Hanna, "Link Wray."
21. O'Hara, "Ventures Guitarist Don Wilson."
22. Prown and Newquist, *Legends*, 22.
23. Moskovitz, *100 Greatest Bands*, 696.
24. Walter Eaton, telephone interview with author, March 6, 2022.
25. Eaton, "Leroy and the Monarchs," in unpublished memoir. Provided to the author by email, March 2, 2020.
26. Walter Eaton, email correspondence with author, March 3, 2022.
27. Though technically not part of the surf-rock oeuvre—having preceded it by three or four years—the Ventures were forerunners and widely considered honorary members, as their sound fit in perfectly. In 1963,

they jumped on the surf-music bandwagon with a version of the Chantays' "Pipeline," followed by an album titled *Surfing*.

28. Singer Johnny Tillotson, who had his own Jacksonville TV show in 1958, recalls a prominent country player named Cecil Jones. Email correspondence with the author, February 23, 2022.

29. Jimmy Amerson, telephone interview with the author, February 19, 2022.

30. Alan Paul, Facebook post, April 16, 2020, https://www.facebook.com/ AlanPaulauthor/photos/one-more-for-duane-betts-birthday-because-its-hard-to-top-this-1990-kirk-west-sh/3150496248334833/; see also Poe, *Skydog*, 69.

Chapter 2

31. Walter Eaton, telephone interview with the author, March 3, 2022.

32. Ibid.

33. Ibid.; Jimmy Amerson, telephone interview with the author, February 23, 2022.

34. Eaton interview, March 3, 2022.

35. Walter Eaton, telephone interview with the author, March 6, 2022.

36. Jimmy Amerson, telephone interview with the author, February 23, 2022.

37. Jimmy Amerson, Facebook message to the author, February 24, 2022; Jernigan, "Cobb Shares History." In an interview with Janet Jernigan, however, Cobb stated he was working as an apprentice welder and was approached by some amateur musicians who worked at the shop and hoped to form a band. Evidently, that was not this band, the Emeralds.

38. Jimmy Amerson, Facebook message to the author, February 24, 2022. A teen group with three guitars was not unheard of. Liverpool's the Quarrymen, the foundation for the Beatles, had three guitarists (Paul McCartney later switched to bass). The three-guitar lineup would later be revived by Jacksonville's Lynyrd Skynyrd and Molly Hatchet.

39. Amerson, Facebook message, February 24, 2022.

40. Mike Pinera, SMS to the author, June 30, 2022.

41. Jimmy Amerson, Facebook message to the author, March 5, 2022.

42. Rick NesSmith, telephone interview with the author, March 2, 2022.

43. Nashville singers were rarely allowed to use their own musicians on recordings; experienced session players would do most if not all the recording work instead.

44. Amerson, Facebook message, March 5, 2022.

45. Nix would later become a prominent session player in Atlanta and drummer for the Atlanta Rhythm Section (alongside Cobb).
46. Brunot, "Robert Nix." The Dynamics had made an impetuous trip to Nashville with a demo tape in 1963 and snagged a deal with Dot Records, which released one single with the group. The single, "Happy Birthday to Julie," didn't do much on the charts, and Dot apparently declined to release a follow-up. Lead guitarist Shink Morris would go on to cowrite several songs, two of which, "Time for Love" and "Rainbow Ride," were performed by Jerry Reed in 1972 and 1973, respectively, and another, "Sleepin' Late," was performed by Dr. Hook in 1977. Nix was playing with the Dynamics at the Golden Gate Lounge on Cassat Avenue in late 1964 when Roy Orbison came in after a concert at the Jacksonville Coliseum and hired him to play with his backing band, the Candymen. Former Dynamics keyboardist Bobby Peterson was already working with the Candymen.

   Music publisher, studio owner and booking agency owner Bill Lowery was pretty much in the middle of everything in the region in those days; music-wise Jacksonville and Tampa were satellites of Atlanta. Lowery had people in Florida, such as Alan Diggs and Paul Cochran, scouting for talent. He even signed Lynyrd Skynyrd—then known as One Percent—to a booking contract sometime around 1967, although how they hooked up with him is not clear.
47. Eaton, unpublished memoir.
48. Ingle's partner at the Golden Gate was Leonard Renzler, who also co-owned a couple of other bars in town, and would become co-owner of the Scene, where a group from Tampa called the Blues Messengers would become the house band in the spring of 1968.
49. Dowopper5151, "Classics."
50. J.R. Cobb, quoted in Jernigan, "Cobb Shares History."
51. James, "Interview with Walter Eaton."
52. Ibid.
53. Eaton, unpublished memoir.
54. White and Williams, *Atlanta Pop*, 48.
55. James, "Interview with Walter Eaton."
56. "Spooky" was covered in England two years later by singer Dusty Springfield and has been recorded dozens of times since, including a rocking 1979 remake by Cobb's band, the Atlanta Rhythm Section.
57. Eaton, interview, March 3, 2022; see also Eaton, unpublished memoir.
58. Mack Doss, telephone interview with the author, April 1, 2016.

59. NesSmith, interview, March 2, 2022.

60. Jimmy Amerson, Facebook message to the author, March 7, 2020.

61. Page Matherson, telephone interview with the author, March 4, 2022.

62. Auburn Burrell, telephone interview with the author, March 7, 2022.

63. Auburn Burrell, email correspondence with the author, May 6, 2022.

64. Burrell, interview, March 7, 2022.

65. NesSmith, interview, March 2, 2022.

66. Burrell, interview, March 7, 2022.

67. Ibid.

68. Hacialioglu, "Morello Talks."

69. Sam Burrell, "Sam Burrell 'Battle of the Blues' 2012 Guitar Center, Englewood, CO 06/05/12," YouTube, June 21, 2021, https://www.youtube.com/watch?v=eisQg1ynm-s.

70. Eaton, interview, March 3, 2022; Hacialioglu, "Morello Talks."

71. Cobb retired to Monticello, Georgia, where he died in 2019.

72. James, "Interview with Sylvan Wells"; see also Poe, *Skydog*, 21.

73. James, "Interview with Sylvan Wells."

74. Wells, "Sally in Our Alley."

75. Actually, the business-savvy members didn't sign directly with Kapp but arranged a licensing deal in which they continued to own the master recordings after the deal expired. It also gave them creative control, and the group insisted on keeping Lee Hazen as its producer. James, "Interview with Sylvan Wells"; see also Poe, *Skydog*, 19–21.

76. Facebook, *Cash Box*, record reviews.

77. McCormack, Facebook post.

78. James, "Interview with Sylvan Wells."

79. "Cowboy Interview," *It's Psychedelic, Baby*.

80. Ibid.

81. The writer's credit was incorrectly attributed to the group members instead of to Dylan.

82. The album was eventually released in 1972 on Alaimo's label, Bold Records, under the title *Duane and Greg* [sic] *Allman*.

83. Bill Pillmore, quoted in FitzGerald, *Roots of Southern Rock*, 171n4.

84. "Cowboy Interview," *It's Psychedelic, Baby*.

85. Brunot, "Tommy Talton."

86. Michael Ray, quoted in FitzGerald, *Roots of Southern Rock*, 171n11.

87. FitzGerald, *Roots of Southern Rock*, 71.

88. Pillmore lives in Asheville, North Carolina, where he operates a small recording studio and continues to write songs.

89. Tasker, "Cowboy: Please Be with Me."
90. Strawberry Alarm Clock "Jimmy Pitman."
91. McCormack, Facebook post.
92. Planer, *Good Morning Starshine.*"
93. NesSmith, interview, March 2, 2022.
94. Kofoed, Facebook post.
95. Jimmy Amerson, Facebook message to the author, March 16, 2022. Pitman, a heavy smoker, died in 2019, after being hospitalized with respiratory failure from COPD.

Chapter 3

96. Rick Doeschler, telephone interview with the author, March 9, 2022.
97. Ibid.
98. Steele, *As I Recall,* 16–17.
99. Ibid., 46.
100. Ibid., 79.
101. Steele, *As I Recall,* 44, 49, 53–54.
102. Ibid., 54 (Dalton Gang quote), 56. Steele mentions the names of many if not most of the Jacksonville teen bands of the era. The list includes about forty bands.
103. Ibid., 38, 64. Students at the school tended to self-segregate by class. The students from the "wrong side of the tracks" were referred to as "hoods" (short for *hoodlums*), while students from the more well-to-do neighborhoods were called "Ortegans" after the upscale Ortega District near the river.
104. Ibid., 75.
105. Ibid., 69; see also Doeschler, interview, March 9, 2022.
106. Steele, *As I Recall,* 69; see also Doeschler, interview, March 9, 2022.
107. Rick Doeschler, telephone interview with the author, March 14, 2022.
108. Steele, *As I Recall,* 75.
109. Ibid., 75–76.
110. Ibid., 82–83.
111. Ballinger, *Lynyrd Skynyrd,* 2–3.
112. Bob Burns, quoted in O'Dell, *Gone with the Wind.*
113. Ibid.
114. Steele, *As I Recall,* 81, 83–84.
115. Ibid., 86–87.

116. Rick Doeschler, telephone interview with the author, March 14, 2022.
117. Steele, *As I Recall*, n.p.
118. Steele's account, as well as Doeschler's, is contrary to many erroneous accounts that claim the group was formed in 1964 as My Backyard.
119. FitzGerald, "One Percent Became Leonard Skinner." The author was in the audience at the Forrest Inn in the spring of 1969, when Van Zant announced One Percent would be changing its name to Leonard Skinner.
120. A list of Lake Shore students would include Ronnie, Donnie and Johnny Van Zant, Rick Doeschler, Larry Steele, Allen Collins, Gary Rossington, Bob Burns, Larry Junstrom, Steve Brookins and Rick Mathews.
121. Steele, *As I Recall*, 57–58.

Chapter 4

122. Reese Wynans, quoted in Paul, *One Way Out*, 22.
123. Mack Doss, quoted in FitzGerald, *Roots of Southern Rock*, 165n1.
124. Dickey Betts, quoted in Aledort, "Big Brother."
125. Ibid.
126. Rodney Mills, telephone interview with the author, July 26, 2022. Engineer Rodney Mills came down from Atlanta to work this session. Mills estimates the date of the recording as August 19, 1968. Betts's singing on this record is notably off-key.
127. Reese Wynans, quoted in Poe, *Skydog*, 72.
128. Randall Hall, Facebook message to the author, March 19, 2022.
129. Gregg Allman, quoted in Paul, *One Way Out*, 2; see also Allman, *My Cross*, 33, 62.
130. Allman, *My Cross to Bear*, 33; Silvertones were not terrible guitars, as they were manufactured by Danelectro. However, their bodies were composed of cheap fiberboard called Masonite. Dan Guitars, "History of Danelectro."
131. Allman, *My Cross to Bear*, 46; see also Poe, *Skydog*, 10.
132. Obrecht, "Bob Greenlee Interview."
133. Poe, *Skydog*, 7.
134. Ibid., 11, 24.
135. Discogs, "*Early Allman*."
136. Sandlin, *Never-Ending Groove*, 64–65.
137. Allman, *Please Be with Me*, 111.

138. Duane Allman, letter to Donna Roosmann in Allman, 2014, 132.

139. There is some question about whether Allman simply showed up at Muscle Shoals uninvited—as producer/studio owner Hall claims he did—or whether Hall summoned him after hearing the Hour Glass recordings. Some sources say Hall sent him a telegram. According to Randy Poe, however, Hall insisted he didn't need another guitarist: "It seems unlikely that Hall—a man in constant motion—would actually take the time to try to track down Allman." Poe, *Skydog*, 77. See also Paul, *One Way Out*, 6.

140. Guitarist-keyboardist Paul Hornsby and keyboardist Chuck Leavell are also from Tuscaloosa.

141. Poe, *Skydog*, 76.

142. Rick Hall, quoted in Paul, *One Way Out*, 6; Actually, Allman's hair was reddish-blond, not white, as Hall stated.

143. Wexler and Ritz, *Rhythm and the Blues*, 225.

144. Ibid.; see also Jerry Wexler, quoted in Freeman, *Midnight Rider*, 33.

145. Duane Allman, quoted in Allman, *Be with Me*, 272.

146. Allman, *My Cross to Bear*, 102.

147. Ibid., 112–13; see also Visit Jacksonville, "Gray House."

148. Ronnie Van Zant's future wife, Judy Seymour, lived a few blocks away on Riverside Avenue in the "Green House."

149. Weiss, "Rossington Celebrating."

150. Poe, *Skydog*, 108.

151. Ibid., 69.

152. Allman Brothers on MV, "Dickey Betts Interview, 11/4/1984 - Rock Influence," YouTube, September 11, 2014, https://www.youtube.com/watch?v=pjTwU9cMrKg.

153. Aledort, "Big Brother."

154. Steve Wheeler, telephone interview with the author, March 12, 2022.

155. A detailed analysis of Betts's style can be found in Zabel, "Betts' Amazing Guitar Style."

156. Dorman, "Dickey Betts"; see also Allman, *Be with Me*, 154; see also Paul, *One Way Out*, 202.

157. Duane Allman had already died in a motorcycle accident by the time of *Eat a Peach*'s release. Gregg Allman didn't exhibit much initiative for taking the reins, so Betts stepped forward as the bandleader.

158. Butch Trucks, quoted in Paul, *One Way Out*, 182–83.

159. Even Burton Averre's lengthy solo on the Knack's 1979 number-one hit "My Sharona" owes a great debt to Betts. Also note that Averre played a Les Paul.

160. Jim Graves, telephone interview with the author, March 13, 2022. Graves worked with ABB drummer Butch Trucks in the late 1970s in a heavily jazz-influenced jam band called Trucks.
161. Wheeler, interview, March 12, 2022.
162. *Rolling Stone*, "One Hundred Greatest Guitarists."

Chapter 5

163. *Road to Jacksonville*, November 2004.
164. Dru Lombar in *Hittin' the Web* (a magazine devoted to Allman Brothers lore), quoted in Simmons, "Damn, Just Damn."
165. Ibid.
166. *Road to Jacksonville*, November 2004.
167. James, "Interview with Dru Lombar."
168. Lovejoy, "Catch a Wave."
169. Lombar told Michael Buffalo Smith he had heard Petty was putting together a group and had gone to Macon in search of him. (Smith, "Lombar Recalls.") However, Central Florida guitarist Larry Howard of Grinderswitch told historian Scott B. Bomar that the group had already offered the position to former bandmate Les Dudek, also from Central Florida. The group was already in rehearsals when Petty and drummer Rick Burnett went to Jacksonville to find Lombar, but it turned out he was in Macon performing with King James Version. Bomar, *Southbound*, 161; see also Brunot, "Grinderswitch."
170. Smith, "Lombar Recalls Grinderswitch."
171. The late Ace Moreland also recorded for King Snake.
172. Dru Lombar in *Hittin' the Web* (a magazine devoted to Allman Brothers lore), quoted in Simmons, "Damn, Just Damn."
173. Smith, "Lombar Recalls."
174. Founding Grinderswitch member Larry Howard has stated that Lombar did not check with the other members before relaunching the group. "He [Lombar] didn't ask anyone what we thought; he just did it." Brunot, "Grinderswitch."
175. Gary Wayne Richardson, telephone interview with the author, July 2, 2022.
176. Steve Wheeler, telephone interview with the author, July 2, 2022.
177. Mary Wilkeson, telephone interview with the author, February 5, 2022.

178. King, "Lynyrd Skynyrd"; see also Ballinger, *Lynyrd Skynyrd*, 41–42. The bass position had already been offered to Jacksonville musician Larry Steele, the author of *As I Recall*. Steele even went to Atlanta to rehearse with the group but found himself edged out by King. The problem was that no one bothered to tell him. Steele, *As I Recall*, 220–27.

179. King, "Lynyrd Skynyrd."

180. Ed King, quoted in Kemp, *Dixie Lullaby*, 75.

181. Wilkeson was also rehearsing with prominent Jacksonville band Running Easy, which included guitarist Randall Hall. He told group members he was returning to Lynyrd Skynyrd. Randall Hall, telephone interview with the author, March 20, 2022.

182. *Down South Jukin'*, "Interview with Leon Wilkeson."

183. Ed King, quoted in Smith, "King of Southern Rock."

184. Kooper, *Backstage Passes*, 179.

185. Whatley, "Clapton Heard Stevie Ray Vaughan." Clapton admitted in an interview, "Every now and then, I just stop and think, 'What [am I] going to do now.'"

186. Scott Sisson, telephone interview with the author, April 30, 2022.

187. Al Kooper, quoted in Everley, "Story of 'Free Bird.'"

188. Kooper, *Backstage Passes*, 180.

189. Steve Wheeler, telephone interview with the author, March 22, 2022.

190. Marty Music, "Ed King's Collection."

191. Dunne, "Does It Have to Be So Loud?" 72.

192. Wheeler, interview, March 22, 2022.

193. Although Hall was hired to play Collins's guitar parts in the revived edition of Skynyrd, King played the solos on "Free Bird." "He knew it note for note," Hall said. Randall Hall, telephone interview with the author, March 20, 2022.

194. Marty Music, "Ed King's Collection."

195. Ed King Forum, "Strats."

196. Smith, *Fender*, 136, quoted in Owens, "Stratocaster Pickup Selector Switch."

197. Jimmy Amerson, telephone interview with the author, April 15, 2022.

198. Scott Sisson, telephone interview with the author, April 14, 2022.

199. Buskin, "Classic Tracks."

200. *Ledger Note*, "What Is Guitar Tone?"

201. Rodney Mills, quoted in Buskin, "Classic Tracks."

202. Kooper, *Backstage Passes*, 192; see also Buskin, "Classic Tracks."

203. Ribowsky, *Whiskey Bottles*, 138.

204. It was in this studio that Ronnie Van Zant and Kevin Elson would produce a set of demos for Molly Hatchet.

205. Joe Kremp, telephone interview with the author, February 12, 2022; Randall Hall, telephone interview with the author, March 20, 2022.

206. Hall, interview, March 20, 2022.

207. Of course, not all Westsiders liked to fight; still, the Westside was arguably the "reddest" part of town at that time.

208. Ed King, quoted in Nunn, "Sweet Home Alabama' Co-Writer"; see also Keel, "Back in Arms."

209. Rock and Roll Paradise, "Steve Gaines."

210. Runtaugh, "Remembering."

211. Beazley, "Moreland Talks."; see also John Moss, quoted in Wooddin and Larimore, "Steve and Cassie Gaines."

212. Page Matherson, telephone interview with the author, March 22, 2022.

213. Moss in Wooddin and Larimore, "Steve and Cassie Gaines."

214. Beazley, "Pyle Talks."

Chapter 6

215. Much of the music Clapton recorded in the 1970s with his new band, of which, most members were from Tulsa, could be categorized as southern rock.

216. Don Barnes, quoted in Bomar, *Southbound*, 229.

217. Matherson, interview, March 2, 2022.

218. Wheeler, interview, March 22, 2022.

219. Matherson, interview, March 2, 2022.

220. Dave Hlubek, quoted in Smith, *From Macon to Jacksonville*, 187.

221. Danny Joe Brown, quoted in Smith, *From Macon to Jacksonville*, 183.

222. Dave Hlubek, quoted in Bomar, *Southbound*, 223.

223. Pat Armstrong, telephone interview with the author, August 22, 2019.

224. Ibid.

225. Kinner, "War over Molly Hatchet."

226. See liner notes by Gail Giddens from Molly Hatchet's debut album from Epic Records, 1978. It seems 38 Special might have been the more obvious candidate, but that group had signed with A&M Records two years before and was in a sales slump from which it would not recuperate until 1979. By this point, southern rock had become passe,

and 38 Special was trying to cultivate a more up-to-date sound and image.

227. FitzGerald, *Roots of Southern Rock*, 136.

228. Steve Wheeler, telephone interview with the author, April 13, 2022.

229. Reiner, *This Is Spinal Tap*.

230. Ron Perry, telephone interview with the author, April 13, 2022. Perry also wrote "Take Miss Lucy Home," which appeared on Hatchet's 1989 album, *Lightning Strikes Twice*, from Capitol Records.

231. Scott Sisson, telephone interview with the author, August 23, 2019.

232. *Kaos2000, "Interview with Dave Hlubek of Molly Hatchet,"* reprinted in Bomar, *Southbound*, 227.

233. Dignity Memorial, "David Lawrence Hlubek."

Chapter 7

234. Mike Bell, telephone interview with the author, April 7, 2022.

235. Meeker, "Mike Campell."

236. Petty Archives, "Mike Campbell."

237. Ibid.

238. Zanes, *Petty*, 59.

239. Mike Campbell, quoted in Baines, "Band Full of Love," 60–61.

240. Bell, interview, April 7, 2022.

241. Ibid.

242. Zanes, *Petty*, 60. Campbell discussed his meeting with the members of the jug band via Bell, who was a part-time member of the group, but did not mention Bell by name. Campbell also said the jam session occurred downtown, but Bell said it was actually in Riverside and was not a commune, as Campbell stated.

243. Rick Doeschler, telephone interview with author, March 27, 2022.

244. Zanes, *Petty*, n.p.

245. Bosso, "Campbell Reflects."

246. Tom Leadon, email correspondence with the author, April 6, 2022.

247. Mike Campbell, quoted in Zanes, *Petty*, 62.

248. Leadon, email, April 6, 2022; William "Red" Slater, email correspondence with the author, April 11, 2022. Slater was the third housemate and took the historic photographs of the meeting.

249. Leadon, email, April 6, 2022.

250. Ibid.

251. Ibid.
252. Ibid. A good case could be made that both "country rock" and "southern rock" were quite similar and in fact part of the same romantic, back-to-the-roots movement spearheaded by Dylan in 1967, along with the Byrds and the Band a year later.
253. Leadon, 2022.
254. DeYoung, "Damn the Torpedoes."
255. Leadon had also gotten into a dispute with club owner Dub Thomas that cost the group a steady gig, and the other band members were understandably irritated. Jourard, "Tom Leadon, Gainesville Rock History."
256. Calder, "Tomorrow of Moons."
257. Leadon, email, April 6, 2022.
258. Zanes, *Petty*, 93.
259. Charile Souza, quoted in Zanes, *Petty*, 95.
260. Uhelszki, "Mudcrutch." Lenahan had been dismissed from the group in 1971, when Petty—and, later, also Roberts—took over lead vocal duties; Jourard, "Jim Lenahan Interview"; see also Zanes, *Petty*, 63; see also Zollo, *Conversations*, 29.
261. Danny Roberts, interview in *Treasure Coast News* sometime during 2007, quoted in Uhelskzi, "Runnin' Down a Dream."

Chapter 8

262. Steele, *As I Recall*, 79.
263. Ibid.
264. There were many future stars in the Cedar Hills section, including guitarists Barnes, Jeff Carlisi and Allen Collins, along with bassist Leon Wilkeson, keyboardist Billy Powell and guitarist-keyboardist Kevin Elson, the latter of whom would go on to have a huge career as a record producer and engineer.
265. Dunne, "Does It Have to Be So Loud?" 6.
266. Pat Armstrong, telephone interview with the author, April 1, 2019.
267. Penhollow, "38 Special."
268. DeYoung, "What's Special."
269. Wirt, ".38 Special Songs."
270. Don Barnes, quoted in Bomar, *Southbound*, 234.

271. Jeff Carlisi, telephone interview with the author, May 25, 2022; see also Banister, *Counting Down*, 73.
272. Everyone Loves Guitars, "Jeff Carlisi Interview."
273. Don Barnes in Bomar, *Southbound*, 234–35.
274. Jim Peterik, quoted in Paulson, "Story Behind the Song"; see also Everyone Loves Guitars, "Jeff Carlisi Interview."
275. Steve Wheeler, telephone interview with the author, April 29, 2022.
276. Jeff Carlisi, quoted in Moseley, "Legendary Les Paul"; see also Everyone Loves Guitars, "Jeff Carlisi Interview."
277. Everyone Loves Guitars, "Jeff Carlisi Interview."
278. Ibid.
279. Carlisi, telephone interview, May 25, 2022.
280. Ibid.
281. Everyone Loves Guitars, "Jeff Carlisi Interview." Carlisi had considered dropping out of college but Ronnie Van Zant advised him to finish his education.
282. Don Barnes, quoted in Parker, "Don Barnes Interview."
283. Wheeler, interview, April 29, 2022.
284. Joyce, "Johnny Van Zant."
285. Smith, "Legends: Blackfoot"; see also Jourard, "Gainesville Rock History."
286. Greg T. Walker, telephone interview with the author, June 30, 2019.
287. Greg. T. Walker, quoted in Smith, *From Macon to Jacksonville*, 88.
288. Walker, telephone interview, June 30, 2019, cited in FitzGerald, *Roots of Southern Rock*, 114.
289. It is not clear at the time of this writing whether founding member Gary Rossington will continue to tour with Skynyrd due to heart problems. Best Classic Bands, "Rossington's Return."
290. Steve Wheeler, telephone interview with the author, June 10, 2022.
291. Steve Wheeler, telephone interview with the author, May 25, 2022.
292. Steve Wheeler, telephone interview with the author, June 11, 2022.
293. Smith, "Bobby Ingram."
294. Ibid.
295. Mike Owings, interview with the author, 2022.
296. Morgan, "Molly Hatchet Celebrates."
297. Derek Hess, telephone interview with the author, June 25, 2022.
298. Greene, "Harwood on Life."
299. Frynds, "Chariot."
300. Greene, "Harwood on Life."

301. Smith, "Drummer Derek Hess."
302. Greene, "Harwood on Life."
303. Ibid.
304. Dale Krantz, quoted in Smith, "Rossington-Collins."
305. Greene, "Harwood on Life."
306. Ibid.
307. Scott Sisson, telephone interview with the author, June 23, 2022.
308. Joe Kremp (drummer for Running Easy), telephone interview with the author, March 10, 2022.
309. Smith, "Randall Hall Interview."
310. Ibid.
311. Ibid.
312. Ibid.
313. Dougherty died in 2008.

Chapter 9

314. Scott Sisson, telephone interview with the author, May 4, 2022.
315. Randall Hall, telephone interview with the author, June 4, 2022.
316. John Kuzweg, "About."
317. Owsinski, "Episode 105."
318. John Kurzweg, telephone interview with the author, July 5, 2022.
319. John Kurzweg, telephone interview with the author, June 6, 2022.
320. Owsinski, "Episode 105."
321. John Kuzweg, "About."
322. Kurzweg, interview, June 6, 2022.
323. Stapp and Ritz, *Sinner's Creed*, 114.
324. Southern Lord Records' website describes Gentry's style as "akin to Hendrix meets Neil Young." Southern Lord Records, "Rein Sanction."
325. Scott Sisson, telephone interview with the author, June 13, 2022.
326. Chase has new music out on https://ianchase.bandcamp.com/album/ian-chase-tony-steve-ep1.
327. Ian Chase, telephone interview with the author, June 17, 2022.
328. Torreano, "Rein Sanction."
329. Smith, "Rein Sanction," 18.
330. Chase, interview, June 17, 2022.
331. Rein Sanction, "Rein Sanction Live."
332. Szaroleta, "Chris Trucks' Life."

333. Steve Wheeler, telephone interview with the author, September 21, 2019.

334. Rick Beato, "The Derek Trucks Interview," July 19, 2022, https://www.youtube.com/watch?v=qMVZtd7XKcQ.

335. Entourage Talent Associates Ltd., "Tedeschi-Trucks Band."

336. Browne, "Trucks Reflects."

337. Kurzweg, interview, June 6, 2022.

338. Steve Wheeler, telephone interview with the author, June 10, 2022.

339. Mayshark, "Ramblin' Man and Woman"; see also Szaroleta, "Chris Trucks' Life."

340. Christ, "Wes Borland Interview."

341. Urban, "22 Most Underrated Guitarists."
Christ, "Wes Borland Interview."

342. Ibid.

343. Ibid.

344. Wheeler, interview, June 10, 2022.

345. PRP, "Limp Bizkit."

346. Filter guitarist Brian Liesegang from Chicago attended the Bolles School in Jacksonville, graduating in 1988. Aside from working with Filter, he worked with Nine Inch Nails.

347. Thiessen, "Borland Speaks Out."

348. Christ, "Wes Borland Interview."

349. Charlie, "Paul Phillips."

350. Wilhelm, "Musicians Discuss."

351. Kurzweg added that PoM singer Wes Scantlin is also a good player and is actually the one who plays the repetitive *wah-wah* solo on "She Hates Me." John Kurzweg, telephone interview with the author, July 5, 2022.

352. Red Jumpsuit Apparatus, "The Red Jumpsuit Apparatus Welcomes Josh Burke," YouTube, July 18, 2011, https://www.youtube.com/watch?v=_2joVqcL3F8.

353. Bialczak, "Burke's Guitar Work."

354. Zaleski, "Note from Ronnie Winter."

355. Red Jumpsuit Apparatus, "Welcomes Josh Burke."

356. McGregor, "Hometown Heroes."

357. Wiederhorn, "Shinedown Get a Leg Up."

Chapter 10

358. Dylan Adams, telephone interview with the author, June 12, 2022.
359. Ibid.
360. Steven Honig, telephone interview with the author, June 13, 2022.
361. Apple Music, "Moving On."
362. Kevin Elson, telephone interview with the author, June 12, 2022.
363. Steve Wheeler, telephone interview with the author, June 11, 2022.

SELECTED BIBLIOGRAPHY

Aledort, Andy. "Big Brother: Dickey Betts Remembers Duane Allman." *Guitar World*, April 2007. Reprinted at Duane Allman Info. https://www.duaneallman.info/bigbrother.htm.

————. "King Albert: Getting a Grip on the Expressive Signature Bending Techniques of Legendary Blues Great Albert King." *Riff*, July 11, 2015. https://riffjournal.com/king-albert-getting-a-grip-on-the-expressive-signature-bending-techniques-of-legendary-blues-great-albert-king/. John Kurzweg. "About John Kurzweg." http://www.johnkurzweg.com/about.

Allman, Galadrielle. *Please Be with Me*. New York: Spiegel & Grau, 2014.

Allman, Gregg. *My Cross to Bear*. New York: William Morrow, 2012.

Apple Music. "'Moving On': Single by Cowford Town Band." https://music.apple.com/us/album/moving-on-feat-peter-keys-single/1453086663.

Baines, Huw. "The Heartbreakers Was a Band Full of Love." *Guitar*, December 3, 2021. https://guitar.com/features/interviews/mike-campbell-blue-stingrays-reissue-surf-n-burn/.

Ballinger, Lee. *Lynyrd Skynyrd: An Oral History*. New York: Avon Books, 1999.

Banister, C. Eric. *Counting Down Southern Rock: The 100 Best Songs*. Lanham, MD: Rowman & Littlefield, 2016.

Beato, Rick. "Will Rock Music Ever Come Back?" YouTube. N.d. https://www.youtube.com/watch?v=ZDivYXthd_c.

Beazley, Tony. "Ace Moreland Talks About Steve Gaines." YouTube. 2001. https://www.youtube.com/watch?v=VkmFR-ibygw.

————. "Artimus Pyle Talks About Steve Gaines." YouTube. August 1, 2007. https://www.youtube.com/watch?v=KnmdyejQYsk.

Best Classic Bands. "Gary Rossington's Return to Lynyrd Skynyrd Stage Following 2021 Heart Surgery." October 23, 2021. https://bestclassicbands.com/gary-rossington-return-lynyrd-skynyrd-heart-surgery-2021-10-23-21/.

Bialczak, Mark. "Josh Burke's Guitar Work Gives Cicero 17-Year-Old a Serious Taste of the Music Life." *Post-Standard* (Syracuse, NY), February 11, 2011.

Bomar, Scott B. *Southbound: An Illustrated History of Southern Rock*. Milwaukee, WI: Backbeat Books, 2014.

Bosso, Joe. "Mike Campbell Reflects on His Long Career as the Rock Guitarist's Guitarist." *Guitar Player*, April 23, 2020. https://www.guitarplayer.com/players/mike-campbell-reflects-on-his-long-career-as-the-rock-guitarists-guitarist.

Browne, David. "Derek Trucks Reflects on Gregg Allman's Life Advice and Legacy." *Rolling Stone*, June 9, 2017. https://www.rollingstone.com/music/music-features/derek-trucks-reflects-on-gregg-allmans-life-advice-and-legacy-195079/.

Brunot, Luc. "Grinderswitch." *Bands of Dixie*, May 2004. https://www.sweethomemusic.fr/Interviews/HowardUS.php.

————. "Robert Nix: Candymen, Atlanta Rhythm Section, Alison Heafner." Sweet Home Music. November 2008. https://sweethomemusic.fr/Interviews/NixUS.php.

————. "Tommy Talton: We the People—Cowboy." *Bands of Dixie* 92 (May 2013). https://www.sweethomemusic.fr/Interviews/TaltonUS.php.

Buskin, Richard. "Classic Tracks: Lynyrd Skynyrd, 'Sweet Home Alabama.'" *Sound on Sound*, January 2008. https://www.soundonsound.com/techniques/lynyrd-skynyrd-sweet-home-alabama-classic-tracks?amp.

Calder, Jeff. "A Tomorrow of Moons: Florida in the 1970s." Jeff Calder's Personal Archive. http://www.swimmingpoolqs.com/jeff-calders-personal-archive/a-tomorrow-of-moons-florida-in-the-1970s/1121692?originalSize=true.

Cartwright, Mark. "Kithara: Definition." *World History Encyclopedia*, June 24, 2012. https://www.worldhistory.org/Kithara/.

Cash Box. Record reviews. October 1965.

Charlie. "Paul Phillips of Puddle of Mudd." Gear Vault. N.d. https://gear-vault.com/paul-phillips-pom-interview/.

Christ, Johnny. "The Most In-Depth Wes Borland Interview Ever." Episode 72. *Drinks with Johnny*. June 21, 2021. https://www.youtube.com/watch?v=PD_W6bK_OBg.

CPI Inflation Calculator. https://www.in2013dollars.com/us/inflation/1969?amount=600.

Dan Guitars. "The History of Danelectro, 1947–2020." https://www.danguitars.com/danelectro.

DeYoung, Bill. "Damn the Torpedoes, Full Speed Ahead." *Bill DeYoung*, July 6, 2015. http://www.billdeyoung.com/music-archives/damn-the-torpedoes-full-speed-ahead-1990/.

———. "Here's What's Special About 38 Special." *St. Pete Catalyst*, December 4, 2019. https://stpetecatalyst.com/heres-whats-special-38-special/.

Dignity Memorial. "Obituary: David Lawrence Hlubek." November 24, 2017. https://www.dignitymemorial.com/obituaries/jacksonville-fl/david-hlubek-7545753.

Discogs. *Early Allman, Featuring Duane and Gregg Allman by the Allman Joys*, Mercury Records, 1973." https://www.discogs.com/release/2145470-Allman-Joys-Early-Allman-Featuring-Duane-And-Gregg-Allman.

Dorman, Jim. "Dickey Betts on Django Reinhardt." YouTube. July 6, 2015. https://www.youtube.com/watch?v=kW-PPvO0MYo.

Down South Jukin'. "Classic Rock Revisited Presents an Exclusive Interview with Leon Wilkeson of Lynyrd Skynyrd." March 11, 2007. https://downsouthjukin.proboards.com/thread/702/interview-leon.

Dowopper5151. "Classics, Who's That New Guy." YouTube. https://www.youtube.com/watch?v=pDEHdMTC3-o.

Dunne, Thomas. "Why Does It Have to Be So Loud?: A Social History of the Electric Guitar." Master's thesis, Hunter College, City University of New York, 2019.

Eaton, Walter. Unpublished memoir. N.d.

Ed King Forum. "Strats." November 27, 2009. https://edking.proboards.com/thread/6/guitars-playing.

Entourage Talent Associates Ltd. "Tedeschi-Trucks Band." https://www.entouragetalent.com/artist/tedeschi-trucks-band/.

Everley, Dave. "The Story of 'Free Bird' by Lynyrd Skynyrd." *Classic Rock*, January 13, 2021. https://www.loudersound.com/features/the-story-of-free-bird-by-lynyrd-skynyrd.

Everyone Loves Guitars. "Jeff Carlisi Interview." November 27, 2020. https://www.everyonelovesguitar.com/2020/11/27/jeff-carlisi-interview/.

Facebook. *Cash Box*, record reviews. Reprinted on "Florida Garage Bands of the 1960s." December 12, 2020. https://www.facebook.com/photo?fbid=10225119282066156&set=gm.10158054919223981.

———. "Florida Garage Bands of the '60's." June 27, 2022. https://www.facebook.com/groups/44851818980/posts/10159183573918981/?comment_id=10159183657668981&reply_comment_id=10159184537608981&notif_id=1656355255211914&notif_t=group_comment_mention.

FitzGerald, Michael Ray. *Jacksonville and the Roots of Southern Rock.* Gainesville: University Press of Florida, 2020.

———. "The Night One Percent Became Leonard Skinner." *Jitney*, August 18, 2021. https://jitneybooks.com/lynyrd-skynyrd/.

———. *Swamp Music: Gator Country's Musical Legacy.* Jacksonville, FL: Hidden Owl, 2018.

Freeman, Scott. *Midnight Riders: The Story of the Allman Brothers Band.* New York: Little, Brown & Co., 1995.

Frynds. "Chariot: Derek Hess—Drums, Percussion." http://www.frynds.com/heartstrings/Chariot/Bios/DH.html.

Greene, Scott. "Barry Lee Harwood on Life after the Rossington Collins Band." Swampland. May 2002. http://swampland.com/articles/view/title:barry_lee_harwood_rossington_collins_band.

Guitar World. "One Hundred Greatest Guitarists of All Time." July 6, 2020. https://www.guitarworld.com/features/the-100-greatest-guitarists-of-all-time/4.

Hacialioglu, Selin Hayat. "Tom Morello Talks About Rage Against the Machine's Self-Titled Album from 1992." Metalhead Zone. February 16, 2021. https://metalheadzone.com/tom-morello-talks-about-rage-against-the-machines-self-titled-album-from-1992/.

Hanna, April. "Link Wray and the Impact of 'Rumble.'" Culture Sonar. May 2, 2020. https://www.culturesonar.com/link-wray-and-the-impact-of-rumble/.

Hynde, Chrissy. *Reckless: My Life as a Pretender.* New York: Doubleday, 2015.

It's Psychedelic, Baby. "Cowboy Interview." April 14, 2015. https://www.psychedelicbabymag.com/2015/04/cowboy-interview-with-scott-boyer-and.html.

James, Gary. "Gary James' Interview with Dru Lombar of Grinderswitch." Classic Bands. http://www.classicbands.com/GrinderswitchInterview.html.

———. "Interview with Sylvan Wells of the Nightcrawlers." Classic Bands. http://www.classicbands.com/NightcrawlersInterview.html.

———. "Interview with Walter Eaton of the Classics IV." Classic Bands. http://www.classicbands.com/ClassicsIVWallyEatoneInterview.html.

Jernigan, Janet. "J.R. Cobb Shares History." *Monticello* (GA) *News*, August 19, 2010. https://themonticellonews.com/jr-cobb-shares-history-p7173-115.htm.

Jourard, Marty. "Gainesville Rock History: The Sixties and Seventies." Facebook. March 3, 2011. https://m.facebook.com/notes/gainesville-rock-history-the-60s-and-70s-bands-venues-stories/bands-bands-bands/159161717470226/?__tn__=C-R.

———. "Jim Lenahan Interview." jpld.com. June 10, 2012. Reprinted on Facebook. https://www.facebook.com/notes/gainesville-rock-history-the-60s-and-70s-bands-venues-stories/jim-lenahan-interview/368711439848585/.

Joyce, Mike. "Johnny Van Zant." *Washington Post*, October 22, 1980. https://www.washingtonpost.com/archive/lifestyle/1980/10/22/johnny-van-zant/91f6897e-2094-4623-9c82-7547484cdde8/.

Kaos2000. "Interview with Dave Hlubek of Molly Hatchet." http://kaos2000.net/interviews/davehlubek.

Keel, Beverly. "Back in Arms: An Interview with Ed King," September 2, 1997. Reprinted in Ed King Forum. https://edking.proboards.com/thread/7/interviews.

Kemp, Mark. *Dixie Lullaby: A Story of Music, Race and New Beginnings in a New South*. New York: Free Press, 2004.

King, Ed. "Lynyrd Skynyrd: Joining the Band." Ed King Forum. November 30, 2009. https://edking.proboards.com/thread/18/joining-band.

Kinner, Derek. "The War over Molly Hatchet." *Folio Weekly*, October 1, 2014, 10. Reprinted at http://folioweekly.com/THE-WAR-OVER-MOLLY-HATCHET,11040.

Kofoed, Preston. Facebook post. August 30, 2019. https://www.facebook.com/photo/?fbid=10218028901226691&set=pob.100000293435664.

Kooper, Al. *Backstage Passes and Backstabbing Bastards*. New York: Billboard Books, 1998.

Ledger Note. "Guitar Guru: What Is Guitar Tone? Understanding and Dialing in Your Sound." August 18, 2021. https://ledgernote.com/columns/guitar-guru/guitar-tone/.

Lovejoy, Heather. "Catch a Wave of Magical Beaches Music of the '60s." *Florida Times-Union*, May 14, 2011. https://www.jacksonville.com/story/entertainment/local/2011/05/14/catch-wave-magical-beaches-music-60s/15903867007/.

Marty Music. "Ed King's Collection | Marty's Guitar Tours." YouTube. August 13, 2017. https://www.youtube.com/watch?v=KnmdyejQYsk.

Mayshark, Jesse Fox. "Ramblin' Man and Woman, Married with Kids." *New York Times*, March 5, 2006. https://www.nytimes.com/2006/03/05/arts/music/ramblin-man-and-woman-married-with-kids.html.

McCormack, James. Facebook post. July 10, 2020. https://www.facebook.com/photo?fbid=903688230129777&set=ecnf.100014658253568.

McGregor, Nick. "Hometown Heroes Red Jumpsuit Apparatus Still Loud and Proud." *St. Augustine Record*, February 21, 2012. https://www.staugustine.com/story/news/2012/02/22/hometown-heroes-red-jumpsuit-apparatus-still-loud-and-proud/16182433007/.

McMahan, Chris. "Don't Be That Guy: Is Sexism Hurting Guitar Shops?" *Reverb*, October 2, 2015. https://reverb.com/news/dont-be-that-guy-is-sexism-hurting-guitar-shops.

Meeker, Ward. "Mike Campell: Still Thrilled." *Vintage Guitar*, July 2017. https://www.vintageguitar.com/32195/mike-campbell/.

Morgan, Lisa. "Molly Hatchet Celebrates 40 Years at Stagecoach 2018." *Coachella Valley Weekly*, April 25, 2018. http://coachellavalleyweekly.com/molly-hatchet-celebrates-40-years-stagecoach-2018/.

Moseley, Willie G. "Two Legendary Les Paul Deluxes." *Vintage Guitar*, October 2017. https://www.vintageguitar.com/32516/two-legendary-les-paul-deluxes/.

Moskovitz, David V. *The 100 Greatest Bands of All Time: A Guide to the Legends Who Rocked the World*. Vol. 2. Santa Barbara, CA: Greenwood Press, 2015.

Newman, Teresa. "The History, Music and Instruments of the Troubadour." Study.com. https://study.com/learn/lesson/troubadour-music-instruments.html.

Nunn, Christina. "'Sweet Home Alabama' Co-Writer Ed King Said Quitting Lynyrd Skynyrd 'Was the Best Thing I Ever Did.'" Showbiz Cheat Sheet. January 31, 2021. https://www.cheatsheet.com/entertainment/sweet-home-alabama-co-writer-ed-king-said-quitting-lynyrd-skynyrd-was-the-best-thing-i-ever-did.html/.

Obrecht, Jas. "Duane Allman: The Bob Greenlee Interview." Duane Allman. 2010. https://www.duaneallman.info/jasobrecht/bobgreenlee/bobgreenleeinterview.htm.

O'Dell, Tom, dir. *Gone with the Wind: The Remarkable Rise and Tragic Fall of Lynyrd Skynyrd*. London: Spritlevel Cinema, 2015.

O'Hara, Marc. "Ventures Guitarist Don Wilson, the Last Remaining Original Member Passes Away." *Unique Guitar*, January 22, 2022. https://uniqueguitar.blogspot.com/2022/01/ventures-guitarist-don-wilson-last.html.

Owens, Jeff. "How to Use the Stratocaster Pickup Selector Switch." Fender. https://www.fender.com/articles/tech-talk/sounds-aplenty-the-stratocaster-pickup-selector-switch.

Owsinski, Bobby. "Episode 105: Labels Negotiate With YouTube, Gibson in Trouble, Producer John Kurzweg." *Bobby Owsinski, Inner Circle Podcast*, April 18, 2016. https://bobbyoinnercircle.com/105-john-kurzweg/.

Parker, Melissa. "Don Barnes Interview." *Smashing Interviews*, October 19, 2011. https://smashinginterviews.com/interviews/musicians/don-barnes-interview-legendary-rockers-38-special-release-live-from-texas.

Paul, Alan. *One Way Out: The Inside Story of the Allman Brothers Band*. New York: St. Martins Griffin, 2014.

Paulson, Dave. "Story Behind the Song 'Hold on Loosely.'" *Nashville Tennessean*, February 21, 2015. https://www.tennessean.com/story/entertainment/music/2015/02/18/story-behind-song-hold-loosely/23646295/.

Penhollow, Steve. "38 Special Holding on Loosely to Their Roots." *Whatzup*, December 21, 2021. https://whatzup.com/music-comedy/38-special-38-special-holding-on-loosely-to-their-roots.

Petty Archives. "Interview with Mike Campbell, September 1999." https://www.thepettyarchives.com/archives/miscellany/interviews/1999-09-mikecampbell.

Planer, Lindsay. "*Good Morning Starshine* Review." AllMusic. https://www.allmusic.com/album/good-morning-starshine-mw0000348275.

Poe, Randy. *Skydog: The Duane Allman Story*. San Francisco, CA: Backbeat Books, 2006.

Prown, Pete, and Harvey P. Newquist. *Legends of Rock Guitar*. Milwaukee, WI: Hal Leonard Corporation, 1997.

PRP. "Limp Bizkit Still Sucks." October 21, 2021. https://www.theprp.com/2021/10/31/reviews/limp-bizkit-still-sucks/.

Rein Sanction. "Part 1 of 2 - Rein Sanction Live - Dickson, TN - July 2020." YouTube. October 3, 2020. https://www.youtube.com/watch?v=IDYRKuPoWCc.

Reiner, Rob, dir. *This Is Spinal Tap*. New York: Spinal Tap Productions/Embassy Pictures, 1984.

Reverbnation Blog. "What the Electric Guitar's Decline in Popularity Tells Us about the Current State of Music." https://blog.reverbnation.com/2018/02/06/electric-guitars-decline-in-popularity/.

Ribowsky, Mark. *Whiskey Bottles and Brand-New Cars: The Fast Life and Sudden Death of Lynyrd Skynyrd.* Chicago: Chicago Review Press, 2015.

Road to Jacksonville, November 2004. http://www.rtjwebzine.fr/rtjenglish/interviews/dru%20lombar%20novembre%202004.htm.

Rock and Roll Paradise. "Steve Gaines, 10/77." October 12, 2015. https://rockandrollparadise.com/stevie-gaines-101977/.

Rolling Stone. "One Hundred Greatest Guitarists." December 18, 2015. https://www.rollingstone.com/music/music-lists/100-greatest-guitarists-153675/dave-davies-41781/.

Runtaugh, Jordan. "Remembering Lynyrd Skynyrd's Deadly 1977 Plane Crash." *Rolling Stone*, October 20, 2017. https://www.rollingstone.com/feature/remembering-lynyrd-skynyrds-deadly-1977-plane-crash-2-195371/.

Sandlin, Anathalee. *A Never-Ending Groove*: *Johnny Sandlin's Musical Odyssey.* Macon, GA: Mercer University Press, 2012.

Simmons, John E. "Damn, Just Damn, Dru Lombar Passes Away." JohnESimmons.com. http://johnesimmons.com/damn-just-damn-dru-lombar-passes-away/.

Smith, Arvid. "Rein Sanction: Rock 'n' Roll Trio Is Polished, Not Slick." *Folio Weekly* 2, no. 14 (July 5, 1988): 18.

Smith, Michael Buffalo. "Bobby Ingram." Swampland.com. February 2001. http://swampland.com/articles/view/title:bobby_ingram.

———. "Dru Lombar Recalls Grinderswitch, Joe Dan and Southern Rock of the Seventies." Swampland.com. June 2001. http://swampland.com/articles/view/title:dru_lombar.

———. *From Macon to Jacksonville*: *More Conversations in Southern Rock.* Macon, GA: Mercer University Press, 2018.

———. "The King of Southern Rock: Ed King Interview." Swampland.com. June 1999. http://swampland.com/articles/view/title:ed_king_1999.

———. "Legends of Southern Rock: Blackfoot." Swampland.com. http://swampland.com/articles/view/title:legends_of_southern_rock_blackfoot/.

———. "The Randall Hall Interview." Swampland.com. July 2001. http://swampland.com/articles/view/title:the_randall_hall_interview.

———. "Rossington Collins Band Drummer Derek Hess: The GRITZ Interview." Swampland.com. February 2009. http://swampland.com/

articles/view/title:rossington_collins_band_drummer_derek_hess_the_
gritz_interview.

———. "Rossington-Collins, the Rossington Band and Lynyrd Skynyrd."
Swampland.com. Summer 2003. http://swampland.com/articles/view/
title:dale_krantz_rossington.

Smith, Richard R. *Fender: The Sound Heard 'Round the World.* San Francisco,
CA: Hal Leonard Publications, 2003.

Southern Lord Records. "Rein Sanction." https://southernlord.com/
store/rein-sanction-s-t/.

Stapp, Scott, and David Ritz. *Sinner's Creed: A Memoir.* Carol Stream, IL:
Tyndale House, 2012.

Steele, Larry. *As I Recall: Jacksonville's Place in American Rock History.* Scotts
Valley, CA: CreateSpace, 2016.

Strawberry Alarm Clock. "Jimmy Pitman of SAC's *Starshine* Album Dies."
August 2019. https://strawberryalarmclock.com/4146/jimmy-pitman-
obituary/.

Szaroleta, Tom. "Chris Trucks' Life Is Steeped in Music, Family." *Florida
Times-Union,* June 14, 2019. https://www.jacksonville.com/story/
entertainment/local/2019/06/14/chris-trucks-life-steeped-in-music-
family/4892752007/.

Tasker, Ian. "Cowboy: Please Be with Me—And Please Remember
Duane Allman." *Here Comes the Song,* October 29, 2021. https://www.
herecomesthesong.com/post/cowboy-please-be-with-me-and-please-
remember-duane-allman.

Thiessen, Brock. "Wes Borland Speaks Out in Support of Marilyn Manson
Abuse Victims." *Exclaim,* February 3, 2021. https://exclaim.ca/music/
article/wes_borland_speaks_out_on_marilyn_manson_abuse_allegations.

Torreano, Bradley. "Rein Sanction." AllMusic. https://www.allmusic.com/
artist/rein-sanction-mn0000391698/biography.

Uhelszki, Jaan. "Mudcrutch: Runnin' Down a Dream." *Scraps from the Loft,*
October 15, 2017. https://scrapsfromtheloft.com/music/mudcrutch-
runnin-down-a-dream/.

———. "Runnin' Down a Dream." *Uncut,* September 2016. https://www.
thepettyarchives.com/archives/magazines/2010s/2016-09-uncut.

Urban, Mark. "The 22 Most Underrated Guitarists of All Time."
Howstuffworks. https://entertainment.howstuffworks.com/the-15-most-
underrated-guitarists-of-all-time.htm.

Visit Jacksonville. "The Gray House." https://www.visitjacksonville.com/
directory/the-gray-house/.

Wardlow, Gayle Dean, and Edward M. Komara. *Chasin' That Devil Music: Searching for the Blues*. San Francisco, CA: Miller Freeman Books, 1998.

Weiss, Arlene R. "Gary Rossington Celebrating Lynyrd Skynyrd 30 Years Strong." May 10, 2003. Reprint *Guitar International*, March 27, 2018. http://guitarinternational.com/2018/03/27/gary-rossington-celebrating-lynyrd-skynyrd-thirty-years-strong/.

Wells, Sylvan. "The Nightcrawlers – 'Sally in Our Alley' (1966)." *A Bit Like You and Me*, June 7, 2013. https://abitlikeyouandme.blogspot.com/2013/06/the-nightcrawlers-sally-in-our-alley.html#story.

Wexler, Jerry, and David Ritz. *Rhythm and the Blues: A Life in American Music*. New York: Alfred A. Knopf, 1992.

Whatley, Jack. "The First Time Eric Clapton Heard Stevie Ray Vaughan." *Far Out*, January 22, 2022. https://faroutmagazine.co.uk/the-first-time-eric-clapton-heard-stevie-ray-vaughan/.

White, Andy Lee, and John M. Williams. *Atlanta Pop in the Fifties, Sixties and Seventies: The Magic of Bill Lowery*. Charleston, SC: The History Press, 2019.

Wiederhorn, Jon. "Shinedown Get a Leg Up from Skynyrd Connection." *MTV News*, April 26, 2004. https://www.mtv.com/news/1486610/shinedown-get-a-leg-up-from-lynyrd-skynyrd-connection/.

Wilhelm, Joe, Jr. "Musicians Discuss First Experience with Law and the Music Industry." *Jax Daily Record*, April 20, 2012. https://www.jaxdailyrecord.com/article/musicians-discuss-first-experiences-law-and-music-industry.

Williams, Alex. "Guitars Are Back, Baby." *New York Times*, September 8, 2020. https://www.nytimes.com/2020/09/08/style/guitar-sales-fender-gibson.html.

Wirt, John. "Classic .38 Special Songs Withstand the Test of Time." *Advocate* (Baton Rouge, LA), April 29, 2013. https://www.theadvocate.com/baton_rouge/entertainment_life/music/article_6e527b6b-ec37-54d2-9d70-c28c96a7133e.html.

Wooddin, Debby, and Jordan Larimore. "Steve and Cassie Gaines to Be Inducted into the Oklahoma Music Hall of Fame." *Globe* (Joplin, MO), September 7, 2018. https://www.joplinglobe.com/news/local_news/steve-and-cassie-gaines-to-be-inducted-into-the-oklahoma-music-hall-of-fame/article_6a3d3f44-71d1-5e38-877f-9d4ef9503ae6.html.

Worl, Gayle. "What Sex Is a Guitar?" *Washington Post*, July 27, 1997. https://www.washingtonpost.com/archive/lifestyle/style/1997/07/27/what-sex-is-a-guitar/1fbd2845-96ec-4000-b442-56aea6996a7b/.

Zabel, Mark. "Dickie Betts' Amazing Guitar Style: Three Simple Keys to Ramblin' Man's Success." YouTube. January 23, 2022. https://www.youtube.com/watch?v=bVMOu7xmwt4.

Zaleski, Annie. "Exclusive: A Note from Ronnie Winter About Red Jumpsuit Apparatus Changes." *Alternative Press*, July 11, 2011. https://www.altpress.com/news/exclusive_duke_kitchens_and_matt_carter_leave_red_jumpsuit_apparatus/.

Zanes, Warren. *Petty: The Biography.* New York: Henry Holt and Company, 2015.

Zollo, John. *Conversations with Tom Petty.* London: Omnibus Press, 2005.

INDEX

ABOUT THE AUTHOR

Michael Ray FitzGerald is a musician, media scholar and former university instructor from Jacksonville. He is the author of four books, including the award-winning *Jacksonville and the Roots of Southern Rock* as well as *Swamp Music*, both of which examine the music and culture of North Florida.

He has a master's degree in media history from University of Florida and a doctoral degree in film and television from University of Reading (UK). He started writing music criticism in the mid-1980s for Jacksonville's *Southeast Entertainer* and went on to write for more than thirty local, national and international publications, including the UK-based *Historical Journal of Film, Radio and Television*.

He is currently working in documentary-film development.

Author onstage with Allen Collins, 1984. *Photograph by Barry S. Miller; used with permission.*